European Theater of Opera

COMBAT

US Infantryman
VERSUS
German Infantryman

Steven J. Zaloga

First published in Great Britain in 2016 by Osprey Publishing,
PO Box 883, Oxford, OX1 9PL, UK
1385 Broadway, 5th Floor, New York, NY 10018, USA
Email: info@ospreypublishing.com

Osprey Publishing is part of Bloomsbury Publishing Plc

Transferred to digital print on demand 2017

First published 2016
First impression 2016

Printed and bound in Great Britain

A CIP catalog record for this book is available from the British Library

Print ISBN: 978 1 4728 0137 1
PDF eBook ISBN: 978 1 4728 0138 8
ePub eBook ISBN: 978 1 4728 0139 5

Index by Rob Munro
Typeset in Univers, Sabon and Adobe Garamond Pro
Maps by bounford.com
Originated by PDQ Media, Bungay, UK

Osprey Publishing supports the Woodland Trust, the UK's leading
woodland conservation charity. Between 2014 and 2018 our donations
are being spent on their Centenary Woods project in the UK.

www.ospreypublishing.com

Author's note

Unless otherwise noted, all photographs are from the author's own
collection. For brevity, in the text the traditional conventions have been
used when referring to units. In both armies, companies were given
identifying numbers or letters that continued through the sequence of
battalions. In the case of US units, A/117th Infantry refers to Company
A, 117th Infantry Regiment, which served in the 1st Battalion; 2/117th
Infantry refers to the 2nd Battalion, 117th Infantry Regiment. In the
case of German units, 2./GR 919 refers to 2. Kompanie, Grenadier-
Regiment 919, which served in I. Bataillon; II./GR 919 indicates II.
Bataillon, Grenadier-Regiment 919.

Editor's note

In this book measurements are given in a mixture of metric and US
customary units of measurement, depending on the context. The
following data will help when converting between imperial and metric
measurements:

1yd = 91.44cm
1ft = 30.48cm
1in = 2.54cm
1m = 1.09yd
1m = 3.28ft
1cm = 0.39in
1mm = 0.04in
1lb = 0.45kg
1oz = 28.35g
1kg = 2.20lb
1g = 0.04oz

Artist's note

Readers may care to note that the original paintings from which the
artwork plates in this book were prepared are available for private sale. All
reproduction copyright whatsoever is retained by the Publishers. All
inquiries should be addressed to:

www.steve-noon.co.uk

The Publishers regret that they can enter into no correspondence upon
this matter.

Key to military symbols

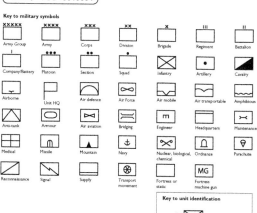

CONTENTS

Introduction

On November 20, 1945, Lt Gen George S. Patton stood in front of a board of 40 senior commanders to discuss the performance of US infantry divisions in the ETO (European Theater of Operations). He remarked that:

A German infantry platoon in the Normandy bocage during the summer of 1944.

The infantry component of the division, which is 65.9% of the total personnel, inflicts on the enemy by means of small arms, automatic weapons, mortars and hand grenades approximately 37% of the [enemy] casualties. In order to inflict 37% of the casualties, the infantry sustains 92% of the casualties of the division.

> The artillery, which compromises 15% of the division, inflicts on the enemy 42% of the total casualties for which it pays but 2%.

Patton's remarks illuminate the challenges faced by infantry in the face of the growing firepower on the modern battlefield. Infantry combat in World War II was haunted by the grim shadow of World War I. The increasing technological pace of machine-age weapons had overwhelmed conventional tactics. Machine guns and rapid-fire field artillery swept the battlefield of unprotected troops. Horse cavalry was no longer viable as the arm of maneuver on the battlefield. The essential ingredient of land combat, the common foot soldier, was slaughtered in ghastly numbers in grim battles of attrition. Tactical and technical innovations in 1917–18 suggested that the era of trench warfare might be a short-lived aberration. At the start of World War II, armored divisions had replaced horse cavalry as the decisive arm of maneuver, changing the dynamics of the battlefield once again. The infantry division had adapted to the new battlefield realities through changes in organization, tactics, and equipment. Infantry could not bunch up and attack *en masse*, but had to disperse, move stealthily, and infiltrate. This led to the "empty battlefield," seemingly devoid of troops.

A typical weapons mix in a US infantry rifle section later in the war, with two soldiers armed with the ubiquitous M1 Garand rifle, the soldier on the right with a BAR (Browning Automatic Rifle), and the section leader with a nonstandard .45-caliber M3 "Grease Gun" submachine gun. The M3 SMG, shown here with two magazines taped together, was intended as an auxiliary arm for tank crews and other vehicles, but was popular in some infantry units as a substitute for the poorly regarded M1 carbine.

The violence and brutality of infantry combat in Europe in 1944 was often hidden in plain sight. While World War I trench warfare might seem to be the epitome of battlefield carnage, World War II infantry combat was enormously costly. Instead of casualties being suffered in a single battle, infantry engaged in sustained engagements over the course of several days or weeks with resulting high rates of loss. During the summer 1944 fighting in France, US infantry regiments on average suffered 100 percent casualties every three months of combat; German casualty rates were usually higher. The ability to sustain units both in terms of morale and manpower, was a daunting challenge to infantry commanders during the war.

It is a common misconception that the fighting in Europe in 1944–45 pitted experienced German divisions against "green" American divisions. This was not the case. The majority of German infantry divisions in France in 1944 were new divisions which had not been in combat. The units may have had small cadres of experienced officers and troops, but they had not fought together in combat until the 1944 campaign. The US Army had a handful of experienced infantry divisions in northern France, but the greatest concentration was in southern France with Operation *Dragoon*, since these units had seen combat in North Africa, Sicily, and Italy.

In comparing infantry in World War II, it is important to examine it at both the micro and macro levels. At the micro level – the squad or *Gruppe* – World War II infantry seems much the same: about the same numbers of troops with some modest differences in weapons. When examined at the macro level, however, at the division, substantial changes become much more evident. This book examines the infantry at both micro and macro levels to better appreciate the differences between German and American foot soldiers in the ETO during 1944.

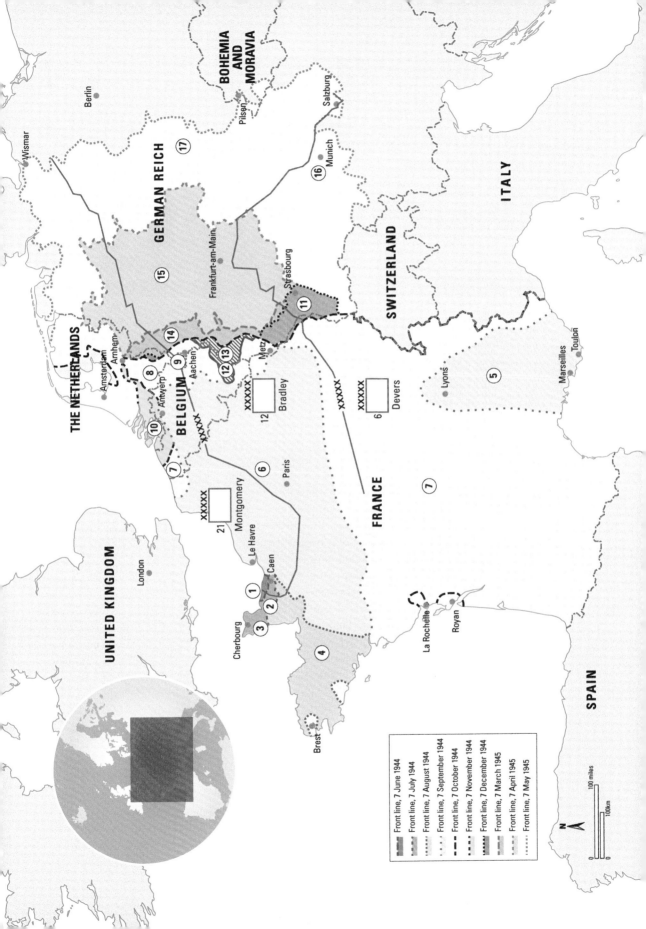

BOHEMIA AND MORAVIA

Berlin

Pilsen

Salzburg

GERMAN REICH

Wismar

⑰

Munich

⑯

Frankfurt-am-Main

⑮

ITALY

SWITZERLAND

Strasbourg

⑪

THE NETHERLANDS

Amsterdam

Arnhem

⑭

⑬

⑨

Aachen

⑫

Metz

⑧

Antwerp

⑩

BELGIUM

XXXXX
Bradley
12

XXXXX
Devers
6

Toulon

Marseilles

Lyons

⑤

⑦

Paris

⑥

XXXXX
Montgomery
21

Le Havre

Caen

FRANCE

⑦

UNITED KINGDOM

London

①

②

③

Cherbourg

④

La Rochelle

Royan

Brest

SPAIN

Front line, 7 June 1944
Front line, 7 July 1944
Front line, 7 August 1944
Front line, 7 September 1944
Front line, 7 October 1944
Front line, 7 November 1944
Front line, 7 December 1944
Front line, 7 March 1945
Front line, 7 April 1945
Front line, 7 May 1945

N

100 miles

100km

The Opposing Sides

ORIGINS AND COMBAT ROLE

German

The German infantry division at the start of World War II was patterned on the assault divisions of 1918. These divisions were large, numbering 17,200 men, 5,375 horses, and 945 motor vehicles. The basic organization centered around three infantry regiments and an artillery regiment. Standardization began to suffer immediately. The infantry divisions were raised in "waves"(*Wellen*), often with modest organizational changes with subsequent waves. The heavy casualties suffered on the Eastern Front in 1941–43 led to the formation of a variety of specialized formations to serve as substitutes for regular infantry divisions in the hopes of preserving the dwindling manpower reserves. In the East, this included security (*sicherungs*) divisions for occupation duty; in the West it included static (*bodenständig*) divisions for coastal defense on the *Atlantikwall*. To complicate matters further, the byzantine politics of Nazi Germany spawned the special ground troops of the Nazi Party, the Waffen-SS, as well as Luftwaffe divisions. These also are outside the scope of discussion here though they saw combat in the West.

In October 1943, the infantry divisions underwent their first major organizational change, originally called the "new style division" (*Division neuer Art*) and in May 1944 renamed Infantry Division War-Type 1944 (*Infanterie-Division Kriegstat 44*). The number of infantry battalions usually decreased from nine to six in one of two configurations: either the infantry regiments shrank from three battalions to two, or the division adopted a two-regiment configuration. In either case, the new binary organization proved awkward in combat compared to the traditional triangular configuration. In the case of the common two-battalion regiment, it compelled the commander to keep both battalions in the line instead of the usual practice of leaving one battalion free

OPPOSITE   A hasty meeting by German platoon leaders in the autumn of 1944, with a *Hauptfeldwebel* (1st sergeant) on the left and a *Leutnant* (2nd lieutenant) on the right. Note that the *Hauptfeldwebel* is armed with one of the new StG 44 assault rifles.

as a counterattack reserve. This was the standard organization at the time of the D-Day landings in the summer of 1944, with the obvious exception of the *bodenständig* divisions. The latter generally maintained the earlier 1943 pattern, but with a greatly reduced number of horses and vehicles. Intended for occupation duty on the *Atlantikwall*, these divisions were allotted substandard personnel. Besides their authorized allotment of weapons, they also had an additional arsenal of weapons associated with the fortifications they manned.

At the start of 1944, the Wehrmacht had 264 infantry divisions deployed in active theaters and another 109 divisions in the process of formation in Germany or on occupation duties. At the time of the D-Day amphibious landings on June 6, 1944, there were about 165 German infantry divisions and 15 other Axis divisions on the Eastern Front. In the West, there were about 90 infantry divisions, with nearly 50 in France and the Low Countries including 25 static divisions, 16 standard infantry divisions and Luftwaffe divisions, and seven reserve divisions.

A third organizational change took place in September 1944 after Reichsführer-SS Heinrich Himmler took over the Replacement Army (Ersatzheer) due to its central role in the coup against Hitler in July 1944. The renamed *Volksgrenadier-Division* was intended to offer maximum firepower with the minimum of personnel and equipment. It was intended primarily for defensive missions on elongated fronts, and was not optimized for offensive missions due to inadequate transport resources. As in the case of the 1944 pattern, the infantry component took one of two forms: either a three-regiment configuration with only two grenadier battalions each, or a two-regiment configuration with the normal three battalions. The *Volksgrenadier* units were supposed to be favored in the appointment of regimental and battalion commanders and assigned young, combat-proven officers with a minimum of the German Cross in Gold, and preferably holders of the Knight's Cross or Iron Cross. These goals usually proved impossible to achieve.

To better appreciate the combat effectiveness of these varying configurations, the three scenarios chosen for this book involve different types of German infantry divisions in combat in the West in 1944. The campaigns of the German Army (Heer) in the West in 1944 were mainly defensive. To offer some variety, one of the combat scenarios selected sees the Heer on the offensive, in the Ardennes in 1944.

American

The US Army infantry division evolved under different circumstances to those of the German division. In the wake of the "War to End All Wars," some senior officers argued that the commitment of the American Expeditionary Force to Europe in 1917–18 was an aberration, and that the infantry should prepare for its traditional missions in low-intensity conflicts such as along the Mexican border and in the Philippines. This type of deployment would present very different demands to those of a high-intensity conflict in Europe or the Pacific. While the infantry was plagued with doubts after World War I, the field-artillery branch emerged as the most vigorous proponent of maintaining the army's ability to wage high-intensity battle.

With war clouds brewing in Europe and the Pacific, the controversy ended. In January 1939, the US Army adopted a new triangular division,

patterned after the German style, in place of the earlier four-regiment structure. Although the US infantry division of 1939 started along a German pattern, it quickly diverged in several critical respects. To begin with, the US Army division had no horses and was entirely motorized. This resulted in a somewhat smaller personnel size: 15,245 men versus over 17,000 men in a German division. Horses require more handlers than trucks, and fodder is bulkier than gasoline. The US division was also smaller, since the Army Ground Forces desired a light and modular unit that could be used anywhere in the world, whether in Europe or the Pacific. Supporting elements that would be needed in different theaters were assigned at corps level and then attached to the division as and when the need arose. As a result, American divisions might seem smaller on paper than German divisions, though often in the field they were significantly larger due to the attachment of tank and tank-destroyer battalions as well as specialized support units.

Each US Army rifle company had a heavy-weapons platoon that included two light-machine-gun sections. They were armed with a tripod-mounted .30-caliber machine gun; in this case, the air-cooled M1919A4 on an M2 tripod mount, shown in action in France on August 28, 1944. The machine-gunner is armed with a .45-caliber M3 "Grease Gun" on his back instead of the more common M1 carbine.

A 60mm M2 mortar section of the 28th Division in action near Perriers-en-Beauficel on August 12, 1944.

The US infantry division was more rigidly standardized than the German. Early experiments such as the light division and motorized infantry division were abandoned before 1944, and all of the divisions covered in this book followed the same table of organization and equipment (TO&E). There were a handful of specialist divisions such as the Airborne divisions and 10th Mountain Division, but they are outside the scope of this book. This does not mean that there were no differences between US infantry divisions, but any differences were based on origins and recruitment rather than structure. The prewar US Army included Regular Army divisions that were raised at the federal level, and National Guard divisions that were raised at the state level and then federalized at the outbreak of war. At the outbreak of war in December 1941, war plans dictated the creation of far more divisions than the existing Regular Army and National Guard divisions, and these were usually raised by combining officers from the Organized Reserves with draftees. All three varieties of divisions are considered in the three combat scenarios in this book. The US Army raised 68 infantry divisions during the war of which 21 were deployed to the Pacific and 47 to the Mediterranean and European theaters.

RECRUITMENT AND TRAINING

German

The Heer recruited on a regional basis through a system of military districts (*Wehrkreise*). Aside from managing the conscription process, the *Wehrkreise* served as the agents for the Ersatzheer to create new divisions and to replenish existing units. At the start of the war, each infantry regiment had a corresponding replacement battalion in its home *Wehrkreis*. For young German men, an initial taste of military service usually began at age 16 with compulsory labor service in the RAD (Reicharbeitdienst, or "Reich Labour Service") which included paramilitary training. Eligibility for conscription started at age 18. Basic training at the start of the war was 16 weeks, falling to 12 weeks by 1942 and eight weeks later in the war; and sometimes only six weeks in late 1944. Technical positions received additional specialist training.

Aside from German citizens, the Heer also accepted *Volksdeutsche*: ethnic Germans living in foreign countries such as Romania, Hungary, and Yugoslavia. Due to the growing manpower crisis in 1943–44, the *Volksdeutsche* category mutated to include draft-age men in various areas absorbed into the Reich such as Alsace-Lorraine and the western provinces of Poland. Most of these draftees did not speak German and this created significant problems. These *Volksdeutsche* tended to be dumped into low-priority divisions; the static divisions on the *Atlantikwall* had a disproportionate number allocated, in many cases as much as 40 percent. The manpower crisis became so serious in 1943 that a program began in the West to substitute so-called *Ost-Bataillonen* (Eastern battalions) for regular German troops. Young Russians, Ukrainians, Georgians, and others "volunteered" to serve in German units rather than starve to death in the horrific German prisoner-of-war camps where millions of Soviet POWs had already died. It should come as no surprise that local German commanders in France were deeply suspicious of

OPPOSITE The Kar 98k rifle was the standard German infantry weapon in 1944–45. The *Landser* on the right has two M39 *Eihandgranaten* (egg grenades) strung from his cartridge pouches.

the combat value of such troops and once again, they tended to be deployed with static infantry divisions on the *Atlantikwall* rather than with regular infantry divisions.

The staggering level of casualties in the summer of 1944 would lead to further manpower improvisations. The most fruitful sources of infantry replacements were the Luftwaffe and Kriegsmarine. The Allied bombing campaign against German oil plants that started in May 1944 forced the Luftwaffe to ground most aviation units except for fighters; the Kriegsmarine likewise tied up most warships except for submarines. These surplus troops were fed into the infantry in the late summer and early autumn of 1944. This was one of the principal reasons for the rapid recovery of the Heer after the summer disasters, the so-called "Miracle on the Westwall." The main problem arising from the hasty repurposing of these troops was that they retained their rank. Luftwaffe NCOs and officers became infantry leaders with no tactical training. Generalmajor Wilhelm Viebig, who commanded 277. Volksgrenadier-Division in the Ardennes, later remarked that "It was easier and quicker to train a young civilian than a Kriegsmarine petty officer who had spent four years on a warship in port and who could not understand why he should die the death of an infantryman in the last year of the war."

Divisions were assessed at four levels of combat value (*Kampfwert*): Kampfwert 1 indicated suitability for offensive missions, while 2 indicated limited suitability for offensive missions; 3 was suitable for defense, and 4 was limited suitability for defense. On D-Day, some regular infantry divisions in Normandy were rated at "1" but *bodenständig* divisions were never rated above "3." After the summer 1944 debacles, most German infantry divisions were rated at "3" or lower.

German divisional sustainment in 1944 was fundamentally different than that for the US Army. The Wehrmacht (German Armed Forces) generally kept units in the field until they were no longer combat-effective. They did not receive enough replacements to remain near their intended strength. As infantry units suffered casualties, they were consolidated into *Kampfgruppen* (battle groups) of smaller and smaller size. In some cases, divisions would receive march battalions from their own *Wehrkreis*, but more often than not, they would be amalgamated with scraps of other units. If not completely destroyed in combat, the division would be withdrawn back to the *Wehrkreis* for disbandment or rebuilding. The three German infantry divisions that took part in the three combat scenarios presented in this book provide a cross-section of the trials and tribulations of raising and training infantry units under the difficult circumstances of 1944.

709. Infanterie-Division (bodenständig) was raised in Wehrkreis IX in April 1941 using older men, and initially served on garrison duty in Brittany. It was transferred to the Cotentin Peninsula in December 1942 where it remained through D-Day. The division was periodically combed for its most able troops who were transferred to the Eastern Front for combat duty. This process left the division with overage troops, soldiers with medical problems, and wounded veterans; in 1944 the average age of its troops was 36 years old. Until the autumn of 1943, it was usually understrength, with only 6,630 troops in June 1943, and had only two regiments. Like other static divisions in Normandy, it had a large number of *Volksdeutsche* troops. Starting in late

The problem posed by the German use of Soviet volunteers is nowhere better illustrated than in this curious pair of photographs. The German photo to the left, taken in May 1944 in Normandy, shows a Georgian *Oberleutnant* (1st lieutenant) of Georgische-Bataillon 795, 709. Infanterie-Division. This officer was a former Red Army general-staff officer, and commanded the machine-gun company in the battalion. The photo below, taken after his surrender to troops of the US 4th Division, shows him describing nearby German troop dispositions.

Gefreiter, Grenadier-Regiment 919

The Heer field uniform gradually became cheaper and less adorned as the conflict wore on. The basic field blouse was nominally in *Feldgrau* (field gray), but this color varied enormously from plain gray through gray-green to a green shade.

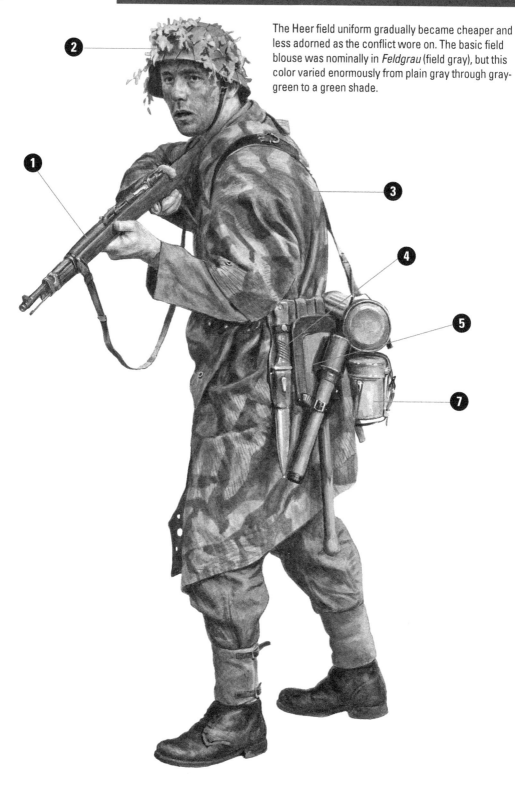

Weapons, dress, and equipment

The standard weapon of the *Landser* was the Karabiner 98 kurz (Kar 98k) (**1**), produced throughout the war. The *Stahlhelm* (**2**) went through several incarnations during the war, and many units in Normandy during the summer of 1944 improvised their own camouflage net from available materials which were then adorned with foliage. Summer evenings in early June could be cool, and many soldiers wore the versatile *Zeltbahn* (**3**) camouflaged shelter-half as a poncho for both rain protection and warmth.

The Modell 84/98 bayonet (**4**) was often worn on the belt for quicker access. The straps on the entrenching tool (**5**) often served as a convenient way to keep a Modell 24 *Stielhandgranate* stick grenade close at hand. The metal gasmask canister (**6**) had been a ubiquitous feature of the German infantry since the later years of World War I. The mess tin (**7**) carried the essential eating utensils and was accompanied by a canteen and metal cup (**8**). Footwear in 1944 was most often a simple service shoe with canvas leggings (**9**). The leather cartridge pouches (**10**) on the belt had a vertical strap to keep them closed using a button underneath, and served as a convenient way to keep a Modell 39 *Eihandgranate* egg grenade (**11**) at hand.

1943, the division underwent a continual string of reorganizations to help prepare it to repel any Allied landings in the area. The most important addition was the transfer of Grenadier-Regiment 919 from 242. Infanterie-Division, raising it to the normal three infantry regiments. In October 1943, the entire I./GR 739 was transferred to the Eastern Front; in early 1944, it was replaced by Georgische-Bataillon 729. This battalion was made up of former Red Army prisoners of war from the Soviet republic of Georgia. Grenadier-Regiment 729 was reinforced with Ost-Bataillon 649, made up primarily of Ukrainian troops. Two more eastern battalions, Georgische-Bataillon 795 and Ost-Bataillon 549, were added in the spring. These eastern battalions were regarded as untrustworthy, and the divisional commander remarked that it was too much to expect that former Soviet soldiers would "fight in France for Germany against the Americans." On May 1, 1944, it had 12,320 men including the *Ost-Bataillonen*. The division had no combat experience, but it was unusually large, with 12 battalions instead of the usual nine due to its overextended defense mission.

183. Volksgrenadier-Division indirectly had its origins in 183. Infanterie-Division, which was created in Wehrkreis XIII in January 1940 from existing replacement and training battalions. 183. Infanterie-Division first saw combat in the Balkans in 1941, and saw extensive combat on the Eastern Front in 1941–44 including the advance on Moscow in 1941, the fighting around Rzhev in 1942–43, and the fighting around Kiev and north Ukraine in the autumn of 1943. In November 1943, it was one of three battered infantry divisions that were consolidated into the improvised Korps-Abteilung C. About half the unit managed to break out of the Brody encirclement on

The *Panzerfaust* antitank rocket launcher came into widespread use as an infantry weapon by the summer of 1944. Although intended for antitank defense, it was often used as a general support weapon. Unlike the larger 8.8cm *Panzerschreck*, the *Panzerfaust* was a one-shot, disposable weapon.

July 24, 1944, consisting of headquarters, services, and support troops. There was an order on July 27, 1944 to reorganize Korps-Abteilung C into 183. Infanterie-Division (Neu) but this never occurred due to the chaotic situation; 183. Infanterie-Division was officially disbanded on August 5, 1944 at Oberglogau in Upper Silesia. Korps-Abteilung C was eventually withdrawn into Austria and on September 15, 1944, it served as the basis for the new 183. Volksgrenadier-Division at the Döllersheim maneuver area. It was immediately amalgamated with the incomplete 564. Volksgrenadier-Division which had been formed only three weeks before. The new division's troops were primarily Austrians who had been deferred from conscription for various reasons. The remainder were mostly Volksdeutsche from Alsace and the western Polish provinces. The unit was transferred to the Westwall starting on September 18–19 with hardly any time for training. As of October 1, 1944, it had an overall strength of 7,791 men, a shortfall of about 3,050 troops.

277. Volksgrenadier-Division was a reincarnation of 277. Infanterie-Division, which had been formed in December 1943 and destroyed in Normandy. The division's remnants that had escaped the Falaise Pocket, about 2,500 men, were sent to Hungary for reconstruction. At the time, the division had only 120 officers, less than a third of the requirement, and only about 1,000 combat troops. Rebuilding as a *Volksgrenadier-Division* began in

Panzerjäger personnel in the *Volksgrenadier* divisions were equipped with 72 *Panzerschrecke* instead of the three 7.5cm PaK 40 towed antitank guns and 36 *Panzerschrecke* found in the 1944-pattern divisions. The *Landser* shown here to the left is carrying a pair of *Panzerfäuste*, while the soldier on the right is picking up his *Panzerschreck*.

mid-September 1944 with plans to have the division battle-worthy by October 10. This was delayed due to a poor supply of replacements who did not begin arriving until October, which led to the division being amalgamated with the new 574. Volksgrenadier-Division. The replacements were mostly young Austrian conscripts who lacked the paramilitary training that was standard in Germany and who in many cases had not received basic training. To complicate matters, there were not enough troops and there was a shortage of equipment. The division moved from its training area in Hungary back to the West to take over the positions along the Westwall in the Eifel region opposite the Ardennes. Additional replacements began arriving from defunct Luftwaffe and Kriegsmarine units. The intention was to continue training the unit once it had deployed but this proved difficult. 277. Volksgrenadier-Division was at 75–80 percent strength at the outbreak of the Ardennes offensive.

American

The Regular Army units were recruited from all over the United States. The US Army National Guard system used regional recruitment in the prewar years, typically recruiting from one or more neighboring states. With the federalization of the Army in 1941, this process stopped and all subsequent recruitment was done nationally. The draft was universal, but in 1944, the Army was still segregated. African-Americans could serve in some types of segregated combat units including tank, tank-destroyer, and artillery, but the infantry was still off-limits except for the 92nd Division fighting in Italy. Draftees were assigned to branch and then sent to one of the numerous training bases. In general, most US infantrymen in 1944 had considerably more training than their German counterparts since the units remained in the United States for a year or more prior to being deployed. US training generally included large-scale exercises at company, battalion, regimental, and divisional level – a type of training that was in very short supply in Germany by 1944. Although well trained, the US Army lacked a significant pool of experienced combat leaders to help impart practical experience to the troops. US Army sustainment policy was fundamentally different than German practice. Units were kept in the field near TO&E strength by providing a steady stream of individual replacements through special replacement depots. At its worst, the replacements were simply fed into the line with no acclimatization. Some divisions soon realized that these new replacements quickly became casualties, and so began programs to better integrate the new arrivals.

The three US infantry divisions involved in the combat scenarios in this book provide a cross-section of the differences in the creation and deployment of US units in the ETO in 1944. As will be noted, all three divisions had ample time for training, frequent opportunities for large-scale combined-arms maneuvers, and all three went into action at full strength. The divisions arriving in the ETO first usually saw action within days of landing; divisions

In the confined terrain of the Normandy bocage, the 60mm M2 mortar provided the US infantry companies with their own "pocket artillery," as shown here during the fighting near Saint-Ouen-des-Besaces.

in the autumn of 1944 were often given a few weeks to break in more gradually, enabling them to build up some basic battle knowledge.

The 4th Division was reactivated at Fort Benning on June 1, 1940 based around three of the oldest regiments in the US Army. It was almost immediately reconfigured as a motorized division. It took part in corps maneuvers in Louisiana and the Carolinas in August–November 1941, and again took part in maneuvers in the Carolinas in the summer of 1942. In April 1943, it was reorganized as a regular infantry division due to the decision to abandon the motorized division concept. After taking part in September 1943 maneuvers, it was moved to New Jersey late in 1943, prior to departing for Europe in January 1944. The division was at reinforced strength when it staged its assault landing at Utah Beach on June 6, 1944.

The 30th Division was reactivated from units of the North Carolina, South Carolina, Georgia, and Tennessee National Guard that were inducted into federal service in September 1940 as one of the first four National Guard divisions. It took part in the 1941 Tennessee maneuvers, and the Carolina maneuvers in October–November 1941. The division lost about 6,000 men that year when one-year enlistments ran out. The churning of personnel was continuous with cadres being extracted to help form new divisions, with the result that the division quickly lost its National Guard flavor as draftees arrived from across the country. The division had a turnover of more than 100 percent in 1942 due to these various factors. The original National Guard commander was replaced by a Regular Army commander, a common practice since senior National Guard officers often were political appointees. In 1943 it took part in the Second US Army maneuvers in Tennessee. The 30th Division departed for Britain in February 1944, landed on Omaha Beach on June 10, 1944, and made its combat debut a day later along the Vire River.

The 99th Division was activated in November 1942, took part in the 1943 Third US Army maneuvers in Louisiana, and arrived in Britain in October 1944. Like many of the newer divisions, it had been stripped of riflemen to make up for shortages in Europe, losing 3,000 riflemen in March 1944. Their places were filled by young men from the Army Specialized Training Program (ASTP). This was an effort by the Army chief of staff, General George C. Marshall, to divert the smartest young soldiers into advanced academic training. At a time when less than 5 percent of young men went to college, Marshall did not want to waste their talents and had them sent to further schooling rather than the battlefield. ASTP came to an abrupt end in 1944 when rising casualties created an immediate need for troops, so 100,000 ASTP college students were transferred to active service. Some were sent as engineers to the secret atomic-bomb program, others to technical branches of the Army, but most ended up as riflemen. The large number of ASTP troops in the division led to its nickname, "Battling Babes." Another feature in common with the late-arriving divisions was the effort made to plug in the unit into a quiet sector for battle acclimation, rather than dispatching it immediately to a "hot" front. The 99th Division was deployed in the Ardennes in November 1944, this being the least-active section along the Westwall. The unit began the routine of patrolling, small skirmishes, and preparing trench-work. Some of the division's forward rifle platoons suffered 30 percent casualties in the second half of November, more than half due to trench foot. Nevertheless, the month along the line prepared it for the shock to follow.

MORALE AND LOGISTICS

German

The Wehrmacht was haunted by the collapse in morale in late 1918 that ended World War I; the Heer in World War II never suffered a similar problem with mutiny and disintegration. This was in no small measure due to policies implemented to avoid a repeat of 1918. In spite of the dire circumstances of 1944, morale in the German infantry remained strong. German society had a stronger military tradition than American society, and military service was widely regarded as both a duty and an honor. Oberstleutnant Günther Keil, who commanded one of the regiments featured in this account, offered a eulogy to his men that expressed the sense of duty and fatalism of the German *Landser*: "The infantry knows no outward honor, they know only their hard duty. With steady gaze, and pale of cheek, they face death in silence. The son follows the father to his fate without complaint. Tireless in the early morning or late at night, dauntless in attack, such is the humble infantry. May God protect you!"

The ability of the Heer to maintain unit cohesion in the face of repeated defeats has been the subjects of considerable fascination. The traditional view has emphasized the importance of a strong level of solidarity within the infantry's primary groups, the *Gruppe* (squad) and *Zug* (platoon). To paraphrase one of the classic studies, as long as a soldier felt himself to be a member of his *Gruppe* and therefore bound by the expectations and demands of its other members, his soldierly performance was likely to be good (Shils & Janowitz 1948: 248). The German replacement system, while it functioned, served to reinforce this by keeping the individual soldier within a close-knit group. Ideological indoctrination by the Nazi Party, while not influential with most soldiers, usually played an important role in establishing a "hard core" group at the center of many units that inspired more determined performance from other soldiers as well as threatening those who did not conform.

Aside from positive reinforcement of morale, the declining fortunes of the Wehrmacht led to greater negative sanctions as well. In the winter of 1943, Nazi Party indoctrination officers, the *National Socialistische Führungsoffiziere* (NFSO), were attached to all military units. These NFSO were patterned after Red Army commissars and were intended to raise morale through political propaganda as well as keep a watchful eye for any signs of defeatism among officers and men. Desertion and defeatism were dealt with more and more harshly in the final months of the war, with increasing numbers of summary executions. In contrast to World War I when 48 German soldiers were executed, in World War II the number topped 20,000.

The German infantry remained dependent on horse transport through the war. This is a Grosser Gefechtswagen Hf 7/11, which had a carrying capacity of up to 1,700kg. The Heer suffered from strained logistics through most of the 1944 campaigns. Although the distances back to the homeland were much less than those endured by the US Army, the Allies conducted continual air campaigns at both the tactical and operational levels to disrupt logistical support including fighter-bomber sweeps in the immediate battle zone, medium-bomber attacks on transportation nodes, and a campaign against rail and fuel into the depths of Germany. Supplies for most units were meager but adequate, though with frequent shortages of artillery ammunition. Beyond the hazards of Allied interdiction campaigns, the Wehrmacht's attention to logistics seldom matched its tactical prowess.

American

In contrast to the average German soldier, the average American saw Army service as a disagreeable necessity. By 1944, the tide of the war had clearly turned in favor of the Allies and most GIs were confident of victory. As in most armies, unit cohesion depended upon small-unit solidarity; a "band of brothers." In his classic study of the Hürtgenwald fighting, Robert Rush concluded that it was "the American army's veteran leaders who were the critical ingredients in US successes" (Rush 2001: 344). Unit morale was the key ingredient in overcoming the natural fear of moving forward in combat and rejecting the natural instinct to retreat or shrink back into a foxhole. As in the Heer, the US Army placed great importance on small-unit leadership by NCOs and junior officers. The test of unit cohesion came quickly for US infantry units in France due to the high attrition rates in the rifle companies. In the summer of 1944, infantry regiments on average were sustaining 100 percent casualties every three months. Most of these casualties were patched up and sent back into the line. In his autobiography, Omar Bradley offered a somber assessment of the infantryman's situation:

> Incentive is not ordinarily part of an infantryman's lot ... He fights without promise of either reward or relief. Behind every river there's another hill – and behind that hill another river. After weeks or months in the line only a wound can offer him the comfort of safety, shelter and a bed. Those who are left fight on, evading death but knowing that with each day of evasion they have exhausted one more chance of survival. Sooner or later, unless victory comes, this chase must end on the litter or in the grave. (Bradley 1951: 321)

The US infantry divisions were entirely motorized, with the General Motors CCKW-353 2½-ton truck being the workhorse of the quartermaster truck companies. The US Army operated more than 3,000 miles from home, yet had developed an extensive and efficient logistical network that kept the units in the field well equipped, especially compared to the Wehrmacht. This was not by chance, but reflected a greater attention to this issue in the wake of the experiences in 1917–18. Although the US Army has often been criticized for having a poor "tooth-to-tail" ratio, it was unique in its ability to sustain large forces at such great distances from its home soil.

By the summer of 1944, the US Army was in the process of switching from the prewar battledress as shown in this plate, to a significantly modified configuration, sometimes dubbed the Model 1943. This involved a shift from the prewar Olive Drab Shade No. 3 colors, which tended toward the khaki/field-drab shades, toward the darker Olive Drab Shade No. 7 colors more in the dark green/olive-drab range. The particular combination shown here would also be typical of North Africa in 1942–43 and Italy in 1943–44. Some of the long-established units such as those serving in the 4th Infantry Division still used the older uniform components.

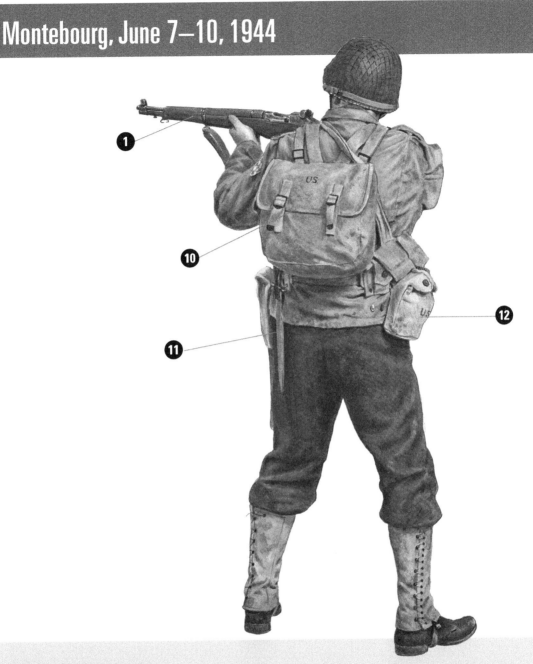

Weapons, dress, and equipment

This man is armed with the standard M1 "Garand" rifle (**1**) with sling. He wears the standard M1 steel helmet (**2**) with one of the several styles of camouflage net, and the Parsons jacket (**3**) in the 1941 configuration. He is wearing the Model 1937 wool serge trousers (**4**). The standard footwear at this point in the summer was canvas leggings (**5**) and the standard brown leather service shoes (**6**).

In preparation for an attack, GIs would usually be instructed to shed any unnecessary gear to facilitate movement, and this GI is shown here only with the bare essentials. The M1923 cartridge belt (**7**) was fabricated from webbing and held ten clips of rifle ammunition; it was supported with the M1936 suspender belt also made of webbing. To supplement this ammunition load, he is also carrying an expendable cotton bandoleer (**8**) which holds a further six clips of rifle ammunition. The M1943 entrenching tool (**9**) could be hung off the belt or attached to the field bag. To lighten the load during combat, the infantry would often leave their M1928 haversacks in the rear and carry only the light assault pack or the musette bag shown here (**10**), officially designated as "Canvas Field Bag M1936" and made of a water-resistant duck canvas. The M1 bayonet was carried in a metal scabbard (**11**) and could be attached to the belt or field bag. The water canteen was carried in the M1941 canteen cover (**12**) and suspended from the belt.

LEADERSHIP AND COMMUNICATIONS

German

The Heer recognized that small-unit commanders were the backbone of infantry in combat. Officer and NCO training was managed by the Ersatzheer in each *Wehrkreis*. Each *Wehrkreis* had one or more *Fahnenjunkersschule* for young officers. There were two routes for NCOs: either through one of the 22 infantry *Heeresunteroffizierschulen*, or through a special ten-week course at a divisional *Feldunteroffizierschule*.

German infantry communications were old-fashioned and relied on traditional methods such as runners and field telephones. The infantry-company headquarters had three runners, one with a bicycle. Although the Heer led the way in radios for command and control at the start of the war, by 1944, they had fallen badly behind. The infantry company was not allotted radios until the October 1943 KStN (*Kriegsstärkenachweisungen*, the German equivalent of TO&E) which authorized two Feldfu b (Feldfunksprecher b). This was a backpack AM radio weighing 13kg (29lb) with a 150mW output and an effective range of about 1,000yd. The December 1943 KStN increased the authorization to four, with usual practice being the allotment of one to each *Zug*. There was a frequent shortage of radios, so many units never even received this minimal amount. The lack of radios hindered command and control in German infantry units during fast-paced actions. Oberstleutnant Günther Keil of Grenadier-Regiment 919 related his impressions during the fighting in Normandy in late June 1944:

> [the Americans] were equipped with excellent portable radios. So the success or failure of an attack could be immediately reported. Before a German company commander received a report by messenger concerning a penetration, the enemy was in a position to bring in additional forces via radio communication, while the German commander was too late in bringing up the weak assault detachments he had in reserve ... a whole hour sometimes passed before a situation report reached my headquarters. Before countermeasures could be applied, another hour would pass and the situation would have already changed.

German tactical radios were larger and less powerful than their American counterparts. The standard small-unit radio was the Feldfunksprecher b backpack AM radio shown here.

American

The US Army used a variety of training approaches to fill out junior officer ranks. The prewar Army had cadres from the National Guard and Officers' Reserve Corps. However, the wartime demands were met primarily by a variety of training programs including Officer Candidate Schools (OCS), and the college-based Reserve Officer Training Corps (ROTC). By 1942, the Army had determined that three months of intensive OCS school was more productive than longer-term ROTC programs, and this became the primary method for preparing the majority of young infantry lieutenants, nicknamed "90-day wonders." The infantry alone required about 36,000 officer replacements in the ETO each month in 1944. As in the German case, the casualty rates among platoon leaders were so great that the practice of awarding field commissions to experienced NCOs increased through the 1944 fighting. As an example, during the seven weeks of fighting in Normandy in 1944, the 90th Division lost an average of 48 percent of its lieutenants every week; the longevity of a lieutenant in a "green" division such as the 90th was two weeks. In contrast to the Heer, the US Army had no dedicated NCO schools, but advanced enlisted men through the ranks within the division.

The US infantry company had a much more lavish allotment of radios, a generation more advanced than their German counterparts. The basic equipment was the SCR-536 "handie-talkie"; a compact, hand-held AM radio weighing only 5lb with a 360mW output and an effective range of one mile. This was less than one-fifth the weight of its German counterpart, with more than double the output. Seven SCR-536s were authorized per company: three in the headquarters including one for the artillery forward observer, plus one in each of the platoons. In addition, it was standard practice for the battalion to provide one of its SCR-300 "walkie-talkie" FM radios to each company for company–battalion communication. Not only was the US allotment of radios more lavish, but units usually had the full authorization.

Communication at company level in the US Army was provided by the advanced SCR-536 "handie-talkie" as well as by more traditional means such as field telephones. This officer of the 117th Infantry Regiment (30th Division) is shown communicating by field telephone, with a pair of SCR-536s sitting nearby, during the fighting around Saint-Barthélemy on August 11, 1944.

ARMAMENT AND TACTICS

Artillery was the primary killer on the World War II battlefield, and the US infantry division's field artillery was significantly better than its German counterpart. As mentioned earlier, Lt Gen Patton attributed 42 percent of German casualties to artillery, but other studies have claimed that it was closer to 80 percent (Comparato 1965: 253). German observers agreed, one senior commander estimating that German field artillery bore 60 to 80 percent of the combat burden by 1943–44 due to the declining combat power of the German infantry (Tholholte 1945: 709). A blunt assessment of the importance of divisional artillery in the infantry battle was offered in 1971 during a lecture at the Fort Benning infantry school by Lt Gen William E. DePuy, an infantry battalion commander in World War II: "what an infantry company really accomplished on any given day was not to 'close with and destroy the enemy' but rather to move its artillery forward observer to the next hill." In terms of weapons, both armies had a similar pattern, with the US division having three battalions of 105mm M2 howitzers, and the Germans having three battalions of 10.5cm leFH 18/40 light field howitzers with similar range and munitions. Each also had a heavy battalion, the Americans with the 155mm M1 howitzer and the Germans with the 15cm sFH 18 heavy field howitzer. Although both sides had similar weapons on paper, there the similarity ends.

Another major disparity was in armored support. All the major armies allotted a portion of their tank force to support the infantry based on the lessons of World War I; the Heer was the exception, concentrating all its tanks in the Panzer divisions. Against the opposition of prominent Panzer leaders such as Heinz Guderian, the infantry finally began to get the industrial resources to build a mechanized version of the 7.5cm infantry gun as the StuG III assault gun. Since production of these competed with that of tanks in the industrial programs, there were seldom enough to go around. They were initially deployed in battalion-sized formations at corps level, and then temporarily assigned to infantry divisions for specific missions. When the 7.5cm PaK 40 towed antitank gun was introduced in 1942, there were complaints that it was too heavy for infantry crews to manhandle. Efforts were then made to adapt it to various obsolete light tank chassis as the Marder *Panzerjäger*. Under the new 1943 KStN, the plan was to deploy a mechanized *Panzerjäger* battalion in each infantry division with a StuG III assault-gun company, a Marder *Panzerjäger* company, and a company of towed

The MG 34 was the standard German infantry light machine gun, gradually supplanted from 1942 by the cheaper MG 42. The tube on the assistant gunner's back to the left is a spare barrel, necessary due to the weapon's high rate of fire and the resultant tendency for the barrel to overheat.

7.5cm PaK 40 antitank guns. So at best, a German infantry division might have had two-dozen armored vehicles attached.

In contrast, US infantry divisions in the ETO usually had a tank battalion and a tank-destroyer battalion attached. These battalions were not organic to the division, but were available in sufficient numbers for semipermanent support. As a result, US infantry divisions typically had four to five times as many armored vehicles in direct support than their German counterparts. The practice was to attach a tank and tank-destroyer company to each regiment, thus substantially increasing its offensive power.

German

German infantry tactics were based around the *Gruppe* light machine gun. Each *Gruppe* consisted of a squad leader (*Gruppenführer*), five riflemen (*Schützen*), and a two-man machine-gun team (*MG Schützen*). The squad leader directed the machine-gun team, and the riflemen were expected to follow their lead. Traditional German tactics usually involved boisterous vocal commands and responses to ensure that all men were firing their weapons and to cement group cohesion further in the chaos of battle. The *Volksgrenadier-Divisionen* were supposed to be armed with the new StG 44 assault rifle, but in 1944, these were seldom available in adequate numbers.

German field artillery had traditionally been very innovative, but fell badly behind due to a lack of communication and computing equipment, a lack of ammunition, poor motorization, and a lack of trained personnel. In 1944, German artillery battalions were often equipped with a grab-bag of standard German types or war-booty captured weapons. Of the formations covered here, 709. Infanterie-Division had two batteries of Soviet 76mm divisional guns, two batteries of Czech 100mm howitzers, three batteries of French 105mm howitzers, and three batteries of French 155mm howitzers. 183. Volksgrenadier-Division had only nine instead of 12 batteries, consisting of four 10.5cm howitzer batteries, two 15cm howitzer batteries, and four 7.5cm gun batteries. 709. Infanterie-Division, since it was static, had no organic traction for its guns except for one battery that had trucks. Most *Volksgrenadier-Divisionen* relied on a mixture of horses, trucks, and tracked prime movers depending on what was available at the given time.

The MG 34 was gradually replaced by the MG 42 light machine gun, though both types remained in widespread infantry use through the end of the war. The MG 42 can be easily distinguished by the stamped sheet-metal cooling jacket over the barrel.

German infantry-division field artillery included three light battalions equipped with the 10.5cm leFH 18/40 light field howitzer and one medium battalion with the 15cm sFH 18 heavy field howitzer, with each battalion having 12 artillery pieces.

15 CM SCHWERE
FELDHAUBITZE SFH 18

10.5 CM LEICHTE
FELDHAUBITZE LFH 18/40

American

The US Army rifle squad was larger than the German *Gruppe*, consisting of 12 men. The standard weapon was the M1 Garand rifle, the world's first semiautomatic infantry rifle. The squad automatic weapon was the .30-caliber BAR (Browning Automatic Rifle) which was smaller and lighter than the German light machine guns, but with a significantly lower rate of fire since it was magazine-fed rather than belt-fed. US small-unit tactics were roundly criticized after the war for not achieving fire superiority over their German opponents. This was in part due to the reliance on the BAR rather than a light machine gun as the basis for the squad's firepower. Most experienced infantry squads recognized their shortfall in firepower and acquired additional BAR or other automatic weapons. The US Army suffered from a "cult of the rifleman," with too much emphasis on carefully aimed rifle fire. In the typical conditions of the "empty battlefield" where the enemy was seldom visible, many riflemen did not fire at all since they couldn't identify a target. One of the Army's observers, S.L.A. Marshall, published a controversial study after the war that claimed only 15 percent of the riflemen fired during combat. This was disputed in 1989 when it became obvious that the study was not based on empirical data as Marshall had claimed, but rather on his impressions. Lt Gen George S. Patton recommended that training be shifted away from an emphasis on marksmanship and that riflemen should fire their rifle from the hip to create suppressive fire when advancing.

In spite of the firepower shortage at squad level, the US infantry company enjoyed firepower superiority at all other levels. The company had an organic mortar section and light-machine-gun section often lacking in its German *Volksgrenadier* counterpart. More importantly, the American company was assigned a radio-equipped forward observer to coordinate field artillery fire. The distribution of field artillery went from about four guns per 1,000 combat soldiers in World War I, to about 23 per 1,000 US soldiers in World War II.

All US divisional field artillery was motorized – a critical factor not only in moving the guns, but also in keeping them supplied with ammunition. US ammunition supplies were nearly always more ample than German supplies. During the October 1944 fighting in Lorraine prior to the assault on Metz, Lt Gen Patton's Third US Army was under ammunition restrictions and yet still managed to fire twice as much as the opposing 1. Armee. The other main US advantage lay in more modern fire controls and more modern fire-control equipment. The US Army had adopted fire direction centers (FDC) before the war that coordinated fires within each battery and linked the battery to battalion and regimental FDC. The ample provision of radios between artillery forward

The backbone of the US infantry division's artillery was the 105mm M2A1 howitzer, with three battalions in each division. This is a battery of the 915th Field Artillery Battalion, 90th Division, pictured on the heights over Winterspelt, Germany, on February 7, 1945 during the Rhineland campaign.

observers and the FDC permitted a timely response to fire requests from the rifle companies. The FDC system also permitted a single FDC to direct the fire of the division's four artillery battalions. The other innovation in fire control was air observation. Starting in 1942, light observation aircraft became organic to divisional artillery. These aircraft could find targets of opportunity beyond the vision of the rifle companies, and were also useful for counterbattery fire against German artillery.

The US Army's organizational improvements led to tactical innovations, the most popular of which was "time-on-target" (TOT). This practice involved the coordination of anything from a single battery up to a coordinated corps-level attack. By calculating the trajectories and ranges of all tubes involved, it was possible to stagger the firing of each gun so that every projectile would land on the target simultaneously. The advantage of this tactic was that it caught German infantry out in the open before they could take shelter. Infantrymen out in the open are about three times more vulnerable than infantry lying on the ground, and more than 20 times more vulnerable than infantry in trenches. A divisional TOT was variously nicknamed a "wreck," "bingo," or "stonk"; at corps level it was called a "serenade."

Besides its 105mm battalions, the US infantry division's field artillery also included a battalion of the 155mm M1 howitzer, as shown here during the fighting in the Ardennes in 1944.

Montebourg

June 7–10, 1944

BACKGROUND TO BATTLE

The 4th Infantry Division landed on Utah Beach on D-Day, June 6, 1944 and proceeded to expand the bridgehead over the next two days. The division's mission was to turn to the northwest and seize the vital port of Cherbourg via

Oberstleutnant Günther Keil's Grenadier-Regiment 919 was raised as part of a normal infantry division and had a solid cadre of combat veterans. This is a ceremony at defense nest W5, on the future Utah Beach, on May 20, 1944, when the divisional commander, Generalleutnant Karl von Schlieben, decorated Leutnant Arthur Janke, commander of 3./GR 919, with the *Ritterkreuz* for his leadership on the Eastern Front earlier in the year.

Oberstleutnant Günther Keil

Hermann Hans Günther Keil was born in Halle-an-der-Saale in Saxony on May 18, 1898. He joined the German Army in May 1917 as an officer candidate with a sergeant's rank in Infanterie-Regiment 147. He remained in the armed forces after the war and was commissioned as a *Leutnant* in 1924. He left the Army in 1925, and joined the state customs service before re-enlisting in the newly christened Heer in 1936.

Keil served in 1. Panzer-Division during the 1940 campaign, and in 256. Infanterie-Division on the Eastern Front in 1942–43. In October 1943, Grenadier-Regiment 919 was transferred from 242. Infanterie-Division to the understrength 709. Infanterie-Division in Normandy. The divisional commander, Generalleutnant Karl von Schlieben, wanted an experienced Eastern Front veteran to lead the regiment, and in November 1943, Keil was assigned to command Grenadier-Regiment 919. Keil led the regiment during the initial fighting after D-Day in the

Utah Beach sector.

During the fighting around the key road junction of Montebourg, Keil was assigned to plan the defenses in this key sector. As his depleted regiment was pushed back toward Cherbourg, it was reinforced with Maschinengewehr-Bataillon 17 and assigned a sector of the Cherbourg Landfront as Kampfgruppe *Keil*. After the fortified Landfront was overcome in late June 1944 by the US Army, Schlieben reassigned Keil to lead the surviving forces on the Jobourg peninsula, the last hold-out force on the Cotentin peninsula. Keil's command bunker in the Kriegsmarine defense nest Wn346 near Digulleville came under fire around 2000hrs on June 30. His artillery commander, thinking that Keil had been killed by an artillery burst near the bunker entrance, raised a white flag. In fact, Keil had survived and in the confusion escaped to the northwest with his driver. He was captured by an American patrol around midnight.

the main road through Montebourg. The division's three regiments were all committed to the advance, with the 8th Infantry Regiment on the left on the western side of the Sainte-Mère-Église–Montebourg road, the 12th Infantry Regiment in the center to the east of the Montebourg road, and the

Colonel James Van Fleet

Born in Coytesville, New Jersey on March 19, 1892, James Alward Van Fleet was raised in Florida before attending West Point, graduating in 1915 alongside Dwight D. Eisenhower and Omar Bradley. An infantryman, Van Fleet served in the US operations against Pancho Villa in Mexico before rising to command a machine-gun battalion on World War I's Western Front.

Van Fleet moved between teaching posts and unit command in the years after World War I. Promoted colonel in June 1941, he became the commanding officer of the 8th Infantry Regiment; unusually, he commanded the regiment for nearly three years before the unit's World War II combat debut at Utah Beach on June 6, 1944, overseeing its combat training in the United States and then Britain. He commented: "The 8th Infantry was a southern regiment, made prior to the draft, mostly of country boys from Florida, Alabama, and Georgia. They were squirrel-shooters who weren't afraid of the dark, who could find their way forward in woods and feel at home. When the draft began, we were filled up with boys mostly from New York, and they brought us the skills needed in a modern army – communications, motorization, mechanization. There was much conjecture as to whether

the Yankees and Rebels would mix. Would there be fights? There were none at all. It was the most happy marriage you can imagine between the north and south into one fine unit that had all the elements a modern unit needs" (quoted in Balkoski 2005: 189).

During the first days of the Normandy battle, Van Fleet's regiment benefited greatly from this continuity, as did the relationship between Van Fleet's unit and other elements of the 90th Division such as the artillery. Having languished for many years owing to a mix-up with another officer with the same name, Van Fleet was quickly promoted as the campaign in Western Europe progressed, becoming assistant division commander of the 2nd Infantry Division in July before becoming first a divisional and then a corps commander.

After holding a succession of senior commands in 1946–48, Van Fleet successfully led the US military team advising the Greek government during the Greek Civil War and then commanded the Eighth Army in Korea. Upon Van Fleet's retirement from active duty as a full general on March 31, 1953, former President Truman called him "the greatest general we have ever had." James Van Fleet died aged 100 on September 23, 1992.

The intervention of tanks of Company A, 70th Tank Battalion would be instrumental in overcoming German defenses in the towns approaching Montebourg. This is an M4 dozer tank named "Apache." Such tanks proved exceptionally valuable in the Cotentin fighting since they could be used to cut gaps in the bocage hedgerows.

22nd Infantry Regiment on the coast, clearing out remaining German *Atlantikwall* defenses. This section examines the mission of the 8th Infantry Regiment to take the high ground west of Montebourg during June 7–10.

The coast in this sector was defended by Oberstleutnant Günther Keil's Grenadier-Regiment 919 of 709. Infanterie-Division (bodenständig). The area around Utah Beach was defended by I./GR 919; this battalion was routed with heavy losses in the first days of fighting. The divisional commander, Generalleutnant Karl von Schlieben, expected that the Utah Beach landing was only the first wave of the attack and that additional seaborne and airborne landings would take place over the next several days farther up the coast on the Cotentin peninsula. As a result, he was reluctant to redeploy the regiment's other two battalions positioned in the beach defenses north of Utah Beach. Behind Grenadier-Regiment 919 was Grenadier-Regiment 1058 of 91. Luftlande-Division; this regiment was committed against the 82nd Airborne Division and the 4th Division in the fighting around Sainte-Mère Église. By the end of June 7, Grenadier-Regiment 1058 had been badly beaten up and its commander killed.

Officers of the 2/8th Infantry inspect an 8.8cm Flak gun of Flak-Regiment 30, part of a German strongpoint on the outskirts of Cherbourg that was overwhelmed by the unit on June 24. They are (left to right): the battalion commander, Lt Col Carlton MacNeely; K/8th Infantry commander, Lt John Rebarchek; and Capt George Mabry, battalion S-3 (operations). Rebarchek was the sole surviving officer of E/8th Infantry after the heavy casualties suffered near Écausseville on June 9. He was recommended for the Medal of Honor for his actions on June 24, later receiving the Distinguished Service Cross instead.

Oberstleutnant Günther Keil led Grenadier-Regiment 919 (709. Infanterie-Division) which faced the 4th Infantry Division at Utah Beach and during the ensuing Cherbourg campaign. A decorated veteran of the Eastern Front, he is shown here with some of his officers prior to the D-Day landings.

A young *Landser*, pictured during the Cotentin fighting in July 1944. He is wearing a camouflage *Zeltbahn*, a shelter-quarter that doubled as a rain poncho. He is armed with the ubiquitous Kar 98k rifle.

Keil was authorized to move III./GR 919 to the Montebourg front late on June 7. The main 7. Armee reserve, StuBtl AOK 7, had been fighting alongside Grenadier-Regiment 1058 on the outskirts of Sainte-Mère Église and it now formed the main defense force along the Sainte-Mère Église–Montebourg road. Commanded by Major Hugo Messerschmidt, StuBtl AOK 7 was one of the best German infantry units in the area. It had a strength of about 1,000 troops and was bicycle-mobile. 709. Infanterie-Division gradually fed in additional infantry units as they became available. Besides the infantry reinforcements, the defenses were reinforced with available corps-level heavy artillery including AR zbV 621 and Stellungswerfer-Regiment 101. On June 8, 10./AR 243 under Leutnant Staalhofer was deployed to Écausseville to establish a defense point along the road. The remainder of III./AR 243 had already been committed to the fighting around Sainte-Mère Église. Staalhofer's battery was armed with four 10.5cm field howitzers and set up a defensive position suitable for close combat. The battery also served as a collection point for stragglers retreating along the road.

MAP KEY

1 June 7: The 3/8th Infantry puts a small detachment over the Coisel Creek.

2 1000hrs, June 8: The 3/8th Infantry commences a day-long battle to secure the World War I airship base and airfield southwest of Écausseville.

3 Morning, June 9: The 1/8th Infantry is stymied south of the Coisel Creek by intense German small-arms and artillery fire in the open pastures northeast of Magneville.

4 Morning, June 9: After receiving false reports that Écausseville had been captured, E/8th Infantry advances forward, but is hit hard by artillery and small-arms fire and withdraws

5 Evening, June 9: Spearheading the 1/8th Infantry attack, Company A, 70th Tank Battalion shoots up German defenses in the Petit Bourg and Grand Bourg farms, and then proceeds to attack Écausseville.

6 Evening, June 9: With darkness approaching and the infantry lagging behind, Company A, 70th Tank Battalion withdraws to the Petit Bourg and Grand Bourg farms on the road intersection east of Écausseville and finds they have been reoccupied by a company from StuBtl AOK 7. In conjunction with the 1/8th Infantry, the US tankers overwhelm the German defenses and about 100 prisoners are taken.

7 Morning, June 10: With support from Company A, 70th Tank Battalion, the 1/8th Infantry advances on Éroudeville.

8 Early afternoon, June 10: The 1/8th Infantry is hit by a counterattack from Kampfgruppe *Simoneit* from the outskirts of Montebourg.

9 Afternoon, June 10: In response to the German counterattack, Company A, 70th Tank Battalion stages a series of raids into Éroudeville, shooting up the town and then withdrawing. During the late afternoon, the tank company withdraws back to Fresville for refueling and rearming.

10 Evening, June 10: The 3/8th Infantry advances to the south of Éroudeville and sets up defenses on the heights overlooking the Le Ham–Montebourg road.

11 Evening, June 10: With Écausseville abandoned the night before, the 2/8th Infantry passes to the west of the village and takes up defensive positions south of the Le Ham–Montebourg road.

12 Evening, June 10: Kampfgruppe *Simoneit*, after halting the advance of the 1/8th Infantry, recovers the survivors of the Éroudeville defenses and pulls back to new defensive lines closer to Montebourg.

Battlefield environment

The terrain south of Montebourg was typical Normandy bocage, with extensive hedgerows protecting the farm fields. The US Army sometimes referred to the bocage as an "inverted trench system" with the solid earthen walls forming a natural fortification system. The area was irrigated by the Merderet River, and there were numerous small streams emanating from it, creating the marshy Cotentin swamps (Marais du Cotentin) in the low-lying areas.

The fighting by the 3/8th Infantry on June 8 focused on this World War I French airship hangar southwest of Écausseville.

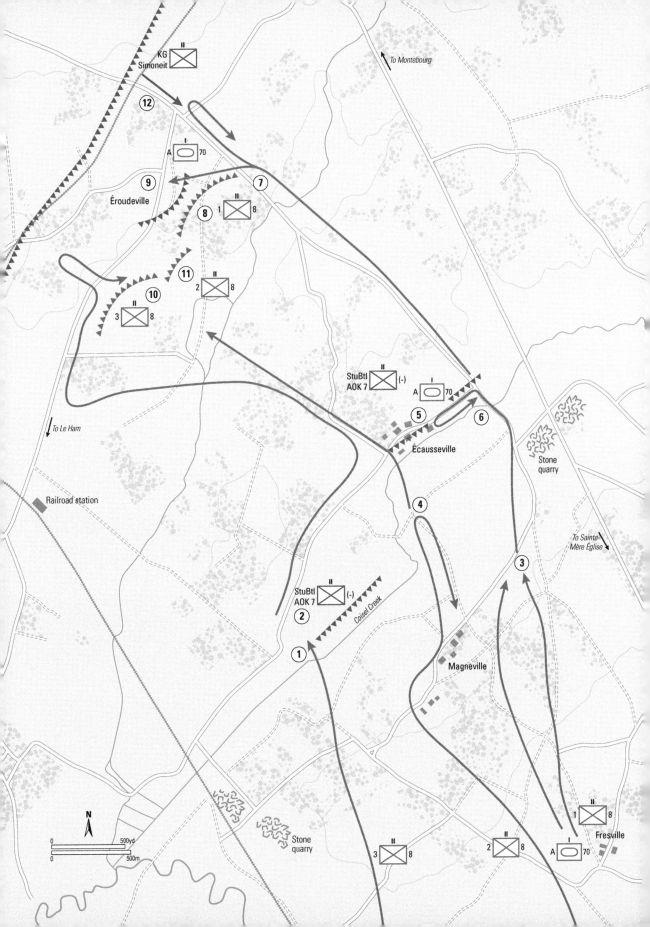

KG Simoneit

⑫

A I 70

⑨ Éroudeville

⑦

⑧ 1 II 8

⑪

2 II 8

⑩ 3 II 8

To Le Ham

StuBtl AOK 7 II (-)

A I 70

⑤

⑥

Écausseville

Stone quarry

④

To Montebourg

Railroad station

To Sainte-Mère Église

③

StuBtl AOK 7 II (-)

② Coisel Creek

①

Magneville

1 II 8

N

0 500yd
0 500m

Stone quarry

3 II 8

2 II 8

A I 70

Fresville

INTO COMBAT

The 8th Infantry Regiment began its swing to the north on June 7 after having secured Sainte-Mère Église. The initial effort was a column of battalions, these eventually spreading out along a front about 2,000yd wide with the 1/8th Infantry on the right, the 2/8th Infantry in the center, and the 3/8th Infantry on the left. German infantry defenses gradually concentrated along the Coisel Creek (Ruisseau de Coisel) that ran diagonally northeast along the US regiment's front. The 3/8th Infantry was the only unit to get troops over the creek on June 7, and one company defended a small outpost over the creek that evening.

There was about a company of German infantry around the French airship hangar southwest of Écausseville, and on June 8, it engaged in a day-long fight with the 3/8th Infantry that the US unit later recorded as having been a "furious battle." The 3/8th Infantry launched its attack around 1000hrs following an artillery and mortar barrage. Three US companies reached the swampy areas on the south side of the creek. German artillery fire along the creek was so intense that the US infantry dubbed the road "88 Avenue." I/8th Infantry, pinned in the creek and suffering casualties from heavy artillery fire, staged a hasty charge across 500yd of open ground, reaching the hangar area. L/8th Infantry was then able to advance into the hangar area and clear the other buildings around the airfield. The 3/8th Infantry set up defensive positions to the north that evening, after having suffered 37 casualties, plus a further ten in the attached heavy-weapons squads. The German infantry was not strong enough to stage any major counterattacks, but was able to slow the advance on June 8. German accounts attribute their success on June 8 mainly to the heavy artillery fire offered by AR 621 and the newly arrived 10./AR 243.

During the morning of June 9, the 1/8th Infantry jumped off from an area of hedges east of Magneville, reaching open fields about 400yd deep. A company from StuBtl AOK 7 was well entrenched on the other side of the

These troops of 709. Infanterie-Division are wearing improvised camouflage at the time of the Cherbourg battle in 1944.

creek in two farmsteads, the Petit Bourg and Grand Bourg farms, that had clear fields of fire over the open pasture. The initial American attempts were thrown back with heavy casualties, and the infantry companies had no means to maneuver against the defenses since the area to the west was exposed to fire from other German units in Écausseville including 10./AR 243. By early afternoon, C/8th Infantry was forced back to its line of departure.

The 1/8th Infantry awaited the arrival of two platoons of M4 tanks from Company A, 70th Tank Battalion. The eight or so tanks led an evening attack up the road toward the farms followed by the battalion in a column of companies. Approaching the Coisel Creek, the tanks began firing on the two farmsteads at the road junction and then turned west toward Écausseville. The infantry did not keep up with the tanks. The German defenders in Écausseville had artillery support, and the US tankers decided against trying to enter the village in the dark without infantry support. The tanks pulled back to the road intersection, where they found that the German infantry had reoccupied the farm buildings. Some more tank fire led to the surrender of about 100 Germans from StuBtl AOK 7, and the 1/8th Infantry dug in for the night. By this stage, StuBtl AOK 7 had been reduced to only about 100 effectives, having suffered nearly 90 percent casualties in two days of fighting. The 1/8th Infantry was down to a strength of 472 men from a starting strength of over 830, even after having received 465 replacements since D-Day. In other words, the battalion had suffered 100 percent casualties in just four days of fighting.

False reports that the 1/8th Infantry had pushed past Écausseville led to orders for the 2/8th Infantry to pull out of reserve and occupy Écausseville. E/8th Infantry led the advance, but came under intense artillery and machine-gun fire as it moved through the fields southwest of the village. The US company, including an attached machine-gun platoon, was reduced to fewer than 75 men after having suffered about 55 casualties; all but one of the

Shortages of motor vehicles led to the widespread use of bicycles for mobility in the Heer during the summer of 1944, including StuBtl AOK 7. This is an example of an antitank unit armed with the 8.8cm *Panzerschreck* rocket launcher.

platoon leaders were among the casualties. E/8th Infantry fell back, and F/ and G/8th Infantry took up the forward position. After a successful delaying action, the battered German infantry and artillery abandoned Écausseville that night. German reinforcements began to appear that evening with the arrival of elements of 243. Infanterie-Division, including II./GR 921, which took up positions on the southwestern approaches to Montebourg.

On June 10, the 1/8th Infantry led the attack with the support of Company A, 70th Tank Battalion. After a preliminary artillery bombardment, some of the 1/8th Infantry mounted the tanks and headed north toward the village of Éroudeville, which had been reinforced by elements of II./GR 912 as well as Leutnant Zobl's 9./AR 243. After an advance of several hundred yards, the US column was stopped by German defenses that included three antitank guns. This time, the 1/8th Infantry closely supported the tanks, and the German defenses were overcome.

The 1/8th Infantry continued forward, and when it reached to about 300yd from the Montebourg–Le Ham road, the American column came under intense fire. This was followed by a counterattack at around 1400hrs by elements of Hauptmann Simoneit's III./GR 919 out of Montebourg that forced back the US infantry. To break up the German defenses, the US tank company decided to conduct raids into Éroudeville without the infantry, conducting five such sorties in which a few tanks charged into the town, fired into the buildings, and then withdrew. By this time C/8th Infantry had arrived on the scene after having served as flank security for the column to the east. With these reinforcements, the 1/8th Infantry finally managed to overcome German resistance. Simoneit pulled back his troops along with the surviving elements of the *Kampfgruppe* from II./GR 921 that had been defending Éroudeville. This fighting also depleted German defenses to the west, enabling both the 2/8th Infantry and 3/8th Infantry to advance to the outskirts of Éroudeville and take the high ground on the Montebourg–Le Ham road by evening. Having accomplished its mission, the 8th Infantry Regiment was instructed to take up defensive positions while the division's other regiments fought their way abreast of Montebourg to the east.

The three-day fight to gain the high ground along the Le Ham–Montebourg road was only a small part of the much larger campaign to capture the port of Cherbourg. The 4th Infantry Division suffered 10,396 casualties in seven weeks of fighting from D-Day to August 1, of which 9,282 were battle casualties. Considering that the casualties fell disproportionately on the rifle companies, most companies endured 100 percent casualties in the June–July fighting. German casualties were equally severe, with StuBtl AOK 7 and Grenadier-Regiment 919 wiped out. The fighting was a combined-arms battle. Field-artillery support was absolutely vital to the German defenses, especially on June 8 when the forward battle line was weakly held. In the American case, the support of tanks on June 9–10 proved to be the essential ingredient in overcoming German defenses when terrain features made maneuver impossible. US tank–infantry cooperation tactics were still in their infancy in June 1944, and innovations in tank–infantry radio communication did not materialize for several weeks.

The Scharnhorst Line

October 2–3, 1944

BACKGROUND TO BATTLE

The First US Army arrived on the German frontier during the second week of September 1944, and made numerous uncontested penetrations of the Westwall fortified line. The border city of Aachen was enveloped from the south, and plans were made to complete the encirclement from the north

A view of Pillbox 5, in the center, from the perspective of A/117th Infantry.

during the first week of October. By this date, the Westwall defenses had been reoccupied and strengthened, so a deliberate assault was necessary. This operation followed standard US doctrine, beginning with an infantry attack by the 30th Division to secure the breakthrough, followed by the 2nd Armored Division for exploitation. This account focuses on a battalion-sized action south of Palenberg on October 2–3, 1944 at the start of the operation.

The 30th Division had suffered 1,680 casualties in September 1944 and had received 1,283 replacements. A/117th Infantry had suffered about 130 casualties in September and was about a dozen men short of strength at the time of the attack compared to a nominal strength of 187 men; the 1/117th Infantry, its parent battalion, as a whole was short about 100 men. A/117th Infantry, under Captain John Kent, had seven days to prepare for the mission, including specialized training in river crossing and pillbox attack. This training was vital as there were many inexperienced replacements in the company, and the assault teams trained in Britain had become casualties in previous fighting. Two specialized weapons were issued for the attack: flamethrowers, and demolition charges mounted on poles. Each platoon had a 16-man assault detachment trained to attack the bunkers. The 1/117th Infantry also sent patrols along the Wurm River to determine the best crossing points. In the days prior to the attack, a battalion of 155mm M12 GMC self-propelled guns fired on the seven pillboxes visible from the American side and claimed 55 hits and 17 penetrations. While the steel-reinforced concrete walls of the German bunkers were proof against 155mm fire, the US guns were able to damage embrasures as well as machine-gun nests and trenches outside the bunkers.

A view inside one of the Palenberg Westwall bunkers after its capture on October 2. The large device on the left is an air-filtration system used to protect the bunker from gas attack, while in the center is a field-telephone set for communicating with the other bunkers.

The unit in the sector opposite the 1/117th Infantry was Grenadier-Regiment 330 of 183. Volksgrenadier-Division. This division had been deployed on the Westwall in mid-September 1944 and had suffered 448 casualties through the beginning of October 1944. It was close to full strength on October 2, with 10,834 troops. Grenadier-Regiment 330, led by Oberstleutnant Hamfler, had only two battalions with a total strength of 1,137 troops. It covered a front about three miles wide, with I./GR 330 under Hauptmann Buhvogel to the immediate south of Geilenkirchen and II./GR 330 under Hauptmann Geisinger covering Übach–Palenberg, the objective of the 117th Infantry Regiment's attack. These forces were deployed in the Scharnhorst Line, the forward line of the Westwall in the Aachen sector in front of the Schill Line farther east. On September 30, Festung-Maschinengewehr-Bataillon 42 was added to the regiment, primarily to man the Westwall bunkers. In the 1/117th Infantry sector, there were nine pillboxes armed with 11 heavy machine guns. The commander of 183. Volksgrenadier-Division, Generalleutnant Wolfgang Lange, anticipated that the main US attack would occur in the northern sector around Geilenkirchen, and so deployed stronger forces there including the division's assault-gun company with 14 Jagdpanzer 38 *Hetzer* ("baiter"). Lange's mistaken appreciation was reinforced by an American deception scheme the day before the main attack, when the 29th Division staged a "demonstration" north of Geilenkirchen.

The plan for the 1/117th Infantry was to strike on a narrow frontage about 1,000yd wide with B/ and C/117th Infantry in the lead and A/117th Infantry in reserve. D/117th Infantry, the heavy-weapons company, was split in two, with half providing fire support in the northern sector and half for the southern sector.

Prior to the attack on the Scharnhorst Line, the 1/117th Infantry prepared a detailed sand-table map of the Palenberg area. Here, the commander of the 1/117th Infantry, Lt Col Robert E. Frankland, discusses the mission with his company commanders. From left to right: Frankland; Capt Clifford Freeman (HQ Co.); Capt John Kent (Company A); Capt Stanley Cooper (Company D); Capt Robert Spiker (Company B); and Capt Morris Stoffer (Company C).

MAP KEY

1 1100hrs, October 2: The 1/117th Infantry leaves the line of departure with B/ and C/117th Infantry in the lead and A/117th Infantry remaining near the line of departure as the battalion reserve.

2 Late morning, October 2: Improvised footbridges are hastily erected over the Wurm River to speed the advance and reduce the vulnerability of the US infantry to artillery and mortar fire. Attempts to put US tanks over the river fail due to the marshy riverbanks.

3 Late morning, October 2: C/117th Infantry suffers heavy casualties to artillery and mortar fire while moving from the river to the railroad embankment.

4 1145hrs, October 2: B/117th Infantry reaches the railroad embankment with modest casualties.

5 Afternoon, October 2: With C/117th Infantry badly hit, A/117th Infantry is ordered to take its place to deal with the pillboxes on the right flank of the battalion advance. It uses the B/117th Infantry footbridge.

6 Afternoon, October 2: 1st Platoon, B/117th Infantry attacks Pillbox 10, then turns its attention to pillboxes 6 and 2.

7 Afternoon, October 2: 2nd Platoon, B/117th Infantry attacks pillboxes 3 and 7.

8 Afternoon, October 2: Hit by small-arms and mortar fire from the vicinity of Marienberg and Palenberg, 3rd Platoon, B/117th Infantry has a hard time reaching its objective but finally overwhelms Pillbox 4.

9 Afternoon, October 2: A/117th Infantry attacks Pillbox 5, then advances on Pillbox 6 which has already been burned out by B/117th Infantry.

10 Afternoon, October 2: A/117th Infantry attacks Pillbox 8, disguised as a farm building, using bazookas.

11 Dusk, October 2: With the line of pillboxes overcome, the 1/117th Infantry sets up a defensive perimeter, expecting a counterattack. A/117th Infantry digs foxholes south of Palenberg, while B/ and C/117th Infantry set up defenses along the edge of town.

12 0330hrs, October 3: Gruppe *Schrader* from 49. Infanterie-Division reaches the outer defenses of A/117th Infantry; two accompanying Sturmpanzer IV *Brummbär* assault guns fire into the defenses and into Palenberg, but are driven off by bazooka fire.

13 After dawn, October 3: The *Brummbär* assault guns return and fire into the woods south of the American defenses, unknowingly prompting the surrender of about 100 troops of Gruppe *Schrader* who had set up defenses there following the previous attack.

Battlefield environment

The terrain in the battle zone was a mixture of open farm fields interspersed with industrial towns and extensive coal mining. As a result, there was an extensive road network through the area, and significant railroad tracks and associated structures. The initial fighting on October 2 took place along the Wurm River in an area which had numerous small woods. It had been raining from September 29 through October 1, and so the ground along the riverbanks was sodden and muddy. The weather on the day of the attack was typical autumn weather, clear and cool. A low front was moving in from the North Sea, bringing some light wind, but the recurrence of the autumnal rain did not reach this area until after the day's fighting.

A view of the 117th Infantry Regiment's attack from the perspective of the German bunkers on the outskirts of Palenberg. This photograph was taken after the attack, with the involvement of a few of the participants to illustrate the unit's after-action report. The railroad embankment is visible in the center of the photograph, as is the church steeple in Scherpenseel where the 117th Infantry Regiment started the attack. The open fields on the ridgeline to the upper right were the location where C/117th Infantry was hit by German artillery fire.

Palenberg

II 330
II ⊠

Marienberg

Valkerhofstadt

Rimburg

Schrader
II ⊠

Wurm River

717
III
119

B 117
I ⊠
B

A 117
I ⊠

C 117
I ⊠

3 B ⊠ •••
2 B ⊠ •••
1 B ⊠ •••

8
1
2
3
7
10
6
5
4
9

① ② ③ ④ ⑤ ⑥ ⑦ ⑧ ⑨ ⑩ ⑪ ⑫ ⑬

2
II
1

N

200yd
200m

INTO COMBAT

The US attack on October 2 began with preliminary air and artillery bombardments, but the air attack was largely ineffective against the bunkers. US field artillery fired about 5,000 rounds that day. The German field artillery was active, but their daily quota was only 20 rounds per 10.5cm light field howitzer and ten for the heavier field guns. After the morning mist had burned off, the US infantry attack started at around 1100hrs. The initial obstacle was the Wurm River, about 15–20ft wide and 3–4ft deep. The two lead companies had the support of divisional engineers to erect footbridges using improvised duckboards and ladders to speed the crossing.

B/117th Infantry was supported by a rolling barrage from the 118th Field Artillery Battalion on the basis of a 100yd advance every five minutes; a forward observer checked the fire when it became apparent that the company was advancing faster than anticipated. Fire support also came from 4.2in and 81mm mortars. B/117th Infantry's sector contained nine pillboxes and about two companies of German infantry. B/117th Infantry was at full strength on October 2 and was commanded by Captain Robert Spiker, an ROTC officer from the University of West Virginia. His commanding officer remarked that "Spiker's virtues as a commander are thoroughness, coolness and a certain quiet efficiency." The 2nd Platoon leader, Lieutenant Don Borton, led the advance over the river, wading across and planting the first ladder to erect a footbridge on the eastern bank of the Wurm. Eleven enemy infantry immediately surrendered at the river's edge, stating that they were Poles and not Germans. During its advance to the river, C/117th Infantry was hit out in the open by German artillery fire and suffered 87 casualties, about half its strength, in the first hour of the attack.

The heavy-machine-gun crews of D/117th Infantry used tracer fire for a more precise attack on the pillbox embrasures, but this revealed their positions and five of eight were knocked out by German mortar fire. The plan to move M4 medium tanks of the 743rd Tank Battalion over the river in support was foiled due to the marshy conditions along the river's edge.

B/117th Infantry begins its advance on the morning of October 2. Palenberg is visible to the left; the mounds are huge slag heaps from the nearby mines. The men of B/117th Infantry hid the duckboards for their improvised bridges in the haystacks on the right.

The 2nd Platoon, B/117th Infantry was on the left flank, and the 1st Platoon on the right. The 2nd Platoon began to engage pillboxes 3 and 7 (designated bunkers 5.3 and 5.2 by the Germans), while the 1st Platoon engaged Pillbox 2 (Bunker 5.604) with machine-gun and 60mm mortar support from D/117th Infantry, deployed along the railroad embankment. While these weapons could cause no appreciable damage to the bunkers, they did persuade many German infantry in the neighboring trenches to escape to the protection of the bunkers. After support squads had been deployed to keep up suppressive fire on the pillboxes, the assault detachments began to move forward to systematically reduce the bunkers. Pvt Brent Youenes, an ASTP replacement, operated the flamethrower against Pillbox 10 (Bunker 5.4), the first pillbox attacked by the 1st Platoon. After Youenes squirted two bursts against the embrasure, Pvt Willis Jenkins ran forward with a pole charge and pushed it through the embrasure opening. A few German infantry survived the blast and at least five surrendered. The 1st Platoon's assault detachment then proceeded north to Pillbox 2 (Bunker 5.604). In the meantime, the US detachment noticed activity to the south at Pillbox 6 (Bunker 5.13) and a team attacked it with satchel charges and grenades. The 1st Platoon's assault detachment changed direction and assisted in the attack on Pillbox 6. Pvt James Smith attempted to burn out the bunker with the flamethrower, but the igniter failed. A German officer rushed from the bunker, killed Smith with pistol fire and was himself shot by the accompanying riflemen.

Pillbox 2 was attacked next, with a pole charge pushed through the embrasure, followed by hand grenades. In the meantime, the 16 men of the 2nd Platoon assault detachment were already attacking pillboxes 3 and 7 (bunkers 5.3 and 5.2). Both were knocked out by pole charges, but the troops in Pillbox 7 were huddled in the relative safety of one of the inner chambers and had to be persuaded to surrender with threats of incineration by flamethrower.

The last bunker to be attacked was Pillbox 4 (Bunker 4.261) which was assigned to the 3rd Platoon, B/117th Infantry. This unit had taken casualties from mortar and artillery fire and its commander wounded. This pillbox proved more resistant than most to attack, with several bursts of flamethrower required through the embrasures, followed by both a pole charge and satchel charge into the rear door. Curiously enough, roughly 15 minutes after the final attack, about ten Germans emerged from the smoldering bunker after the ammunition inside began to "cook off." The B/117th Infantry assault detachments suffered two killed and eight wounded in the reduction of the pillboxes, while the 3rd Platoon and Weapons Platoon suffered one killed and 18 wounded. German casualties were not recorded but were in excess of 100 killed, captured, and wounded. A US after-action report later recounted that "The quality of the opposing infantry troops was mixed; there were some fanatics sprinkled through the lot, but many were old or young men, some decrepit or bewildered, and most seemed willing to surrender after a brief show of resistance."

Since C/117th Infantry had suffered such high casualties in the advance to the river, the regimental commander, Lt Col Robert E. Frankland, decided to commit his reserve, Capt John E. Kent's A/117th Infantry, to take over C/117th Infantry's mission. A/117th Infantry advanced to the river in a column of platoons led by the 2nd Platoon. As they approached the river, they began to receive artillery fire and so Kent ordered the company to shift to the right and into the 3rd Platoon's sector under the cover of a wooded area. Kent ordered Lt Johnston, the 2nd Platoon leader, to deal with the pillboxes once they moved over the river. Johnston was an air cadet who had only recently been transferred to the infantry and he had depended on the platoon sergeant, T/Sgt Revier, who had been wounded by artillery fire earlier that day. Johnston told Kent he wasn't qualified to lead the platoon on the mission. Kent instead turned to the 3rd Platoon leader, Lt Theodore Foote, and ordered him to take pillboxes 5 and 6.

Born in Stephens, Texas, in 1924, Foote had joined A/117th Infantry in August 1944. When interviewed by a combat historian after the Scharnhorst Line fighting, he outlined his leadership principle: "You can't push a string, you have to pull it." His commanding officer later described him:

> Foote does not look like a leader; he is a short, slimly built boy with a high voice. He sounds afraid of his own shadow, and lacks all the bluster sometimes associated with those who hail from his area of Texas. He is a young officer, only 11 months out of Fort Benning OCS [Officer Candidate School]. He leads his men by the simple principle of example.

A/117th Infantry emerged from the woods and rapidly raced to the river's edge. German artillery fire began to fall on the woods, but too late to have much effect. There was sporadic machine-gun fire in the three minutes it took the US company to reach the river. A/117th Infantry advanced over the river using the B/117th Infantry footbridge and reached the railroad embankment on the opposite side in another three minutes, suffering most of its casualties in the process due to the machine-gun fire from the bunkers and the surrounding weapons pits, as well as from German positions farther to the south. Foote led the 3rd Platoon over the railroad embankment, urging the men to fire as they advanced.

The 3rd Platoon concentrated on Pillbox 5 (Bunker 5.18) and two fire-support teams brought the German defenses under fire from BARs and rifles. Prior to the attack, the flamethrower operator indicated that the device would not work; a common problem with the balky M1A1 flamethrower. Foote led six men of the assault detachment against Pillbox 5. The detachment's principal weapons for bunker attacks were a pole charge handled by Pvt Marvin Sirokin and a bazooka handled by Pfc Gus Pantazopulos. The 38-year-old Greek immigrant had trained on bazookas at the Fort Hood tank-destroyer school before being transferred to the infantry. He was very fond of the bazooka and well versed in its operation. Pantazopulos crawled to within 20ft of the bunker embrasures and fired one rocket against each of the two embrasures. The rocket that struck the western embrasure tore an opening in the steel plate. Before the smoke settled, Sirokin raced from his hiding place in a shell crater near the bunker and thrust the pole charge through the opening. After the explosion, the rest of the detachment raced forward to the bunker to throw grenades inside. Foote was wounded in the face when a surviving German in the bunker threw out a grenade. The platoon sergeant, T/Sgt Francis Banner, took temporary command of the platoon until Foote recovered his senses from the blast.

The bazooka team of 3rd Platoon, A/117th Infantry, credited with knocking out the pillboxes, consisted of the bazooka gunner, Pfc Gus Pantazopulos, with Cpl Russell Martin loading.

The fight for Pillbox 5

German view: Pillbox 5 (Bunker 5.18) was manned by specialized troops of Festung-Maschinengewehr-Bataillon 42. These units were hastily organized in the late summer of 1944 to man the Westwall bunkers after years of neglect. They were necessary also because the embrasures of the bunkers would not accept the new MG 42 light machine gun's barrel, whereas these units had older types of machine guns suitable for use in the bunkers. Pillbox 5 was a double-embrasure bunker, though its specific version is not recorded. These bunkers had two fighting rooms for the machine guns, and included a separate living quarters for the troops. This bunker was netted to other bunkers through a field telephone, also used to communicate with neighboring artillery units. The troops on the exterior of the bunker were from II./GR 330 under Hauptmann Geisinger. German tactical doctrine recognized the value of bunkers in providing shelter for troops during preliminary enemy artillery bombardment, but once the infantry closed on the bunker, the role of the infantry troops was to exit the bunker and defend it from trenches nearby. There was about a squad of infantry in the immediate vicinity of the bunker on October 2, 1944, including at least two machine-gun positions. One of the problems for the Germans on October 2 was that the inexperienced German infantry took shelter in the bunkers rather than remaining outside to defend them.

American view: Lt Theodore Foote's 3rd Platoon, A/117th Infantry concentrated on Pillbox 5. Foote's men were supported by .30-caliber machine guns and 60mm mortars from D/117th Infantry, the battalion's heavy-weapons company. Sgt Underwood moved his fire team closer and deployed a BAR and riflemen to provide suppressive fire while Cpl Tripplett of the left-side fire team concentrated his unit's fire against the pillbox embrasures. Under this cover fire, the demolition detachment under Lt Foote moved closer, using the cover of shell craters and terrain to advance to within 20–30yd of the bunker. When in range, Pfc Gus Pantazopulos fired bazooka rockets against each of the two embrasures, and as the smoke settled, Pvt Sirokin raced from his hiding place in a shell crater near the bunker and thrust a pole charge through the opening. After the explosion, the rest of the detachment rushed forward to the bunker to throw grenades inside. Other members of the platoon assaulted the neighboring trenches to root out the German defenders.

The next objective was Pillbox 8 (Bunker 10) which was disguised as a farm building. Foote's 3rd Platoon, reinforced by some men from C/117th Infantry, were brought under fire from German mortars. The assault detachment moved forward again, and Pantazopulos broke open the pillbox with two more bazooka rockets. At dusk, A/117th Infantry deployed in a defensive line south of Palenberg in anticipation of the predictable German counterattack. Capt Kent set up headquarters in one of the Westwall bunkers, but this proved to be a mixed blessing as the Germans kept striking the roof of the bunker through the night with fire from a nearby 3.7cm FlaK autocannon. Kent was reluctant to call in artillery fire against the woods where the gun was located as there were reports that US troops were in the area as well.

Late on October 2, 183. Volksgrenadier-Division was ordered to regain the Westwall and to push the 30th Division back over the Wurm River. Since the penetration by the 117th Infantry Regiment had occurred along the divisional boundary, the neighboring 49. Infanterie-Division to the south was ordered to provide a battalion-sized force, Gruppe *Schrader*, based around three companies of Grenadier-Regiment 148. Gruppe *Schrader* attacked from the south, with the support of a few Sturmpanzer IV *Brummbär* assault guns of StuPzAbt 217. Elements of Gruppe *Schrader* hit A/117th Infantry in the early-morning hours of October 3. Two *Brummbär* assault guns with about 20 accompanying infantry advanced to within a few feet of the outer foxholes

German prisoners from the fighting on October 2 are collected in a courtyard in Palenberg by troops of the 117th Infantry Regiment.

The
assault detachment of 3rd
Platoon, A/117th Infantry,
photographed days after the
attack. Lt Theodore Foote is in
the center of the rear row. He
was later decorated with the
Silver Star for his leadership
during the Palenberg fighting.

and began firing toward Palenberg. Bazooka teams deeper in the defenses hit one of the assault guns, causing it to withdraw abruptly. Seven German infantrymen were killed and the assault guns pulled back and continued firing at the foxholes with their machine guns until dissuaded by more bazooka fire. The assault guns remained in the area after the failed attack, and after dawn, they fired into a nearby wood, leading to the surrender of about 100 German troops to the surprised American defenders. The American after-action report noted that this force could have overrun A/117th Infantry the night before if the attack had been coordinated with the other elements of Gruppe *Schrader*.

Gruppe *Schrader* lost about 100 troops during the attack, including about 80 prisoners from 5./IR 148. The 30th Division captured a further 184 troops from Grenadier-Regiment 330 by the end of October 3. A total of 1,042 soldiers were captured from 183. Volksgrenadier-Division as well as 883 from 49. Infanterie-Division through October 7. The casualties of A/117th Infantry were one killed and 15 wounded on October 2 and 13 wounded on October 3. Casualties in the 117th Infantry Regiment were 473 through October 7.

The fighting on the Scharnhorst Line on October 2 was only the start of the second battle of Aachen. The encirclement of the city took two weeks of intense combat and was not complete until October 16. Aachen fell to the US Army on October 21, the first German city lost to the Allies. The successful penetration of the Scharnhorst Line on October 2–3 was due to the prudent tactics employed by an experienced American division. The officers of the 117th Infantry Regiment fully understood that the Germans had preregistered the Wurm River and other key points, and that the only way to minimize artillery casualties was to move swiftly before German forward observers could shift fires onto them. This tactic mostly succeeded, except in the case of C/117th Infantry. The US assault tactics against the pillboxes proved effective due to realistic training and the success of the field artillery and crew-served heavy weapons in forcing the German infantry into the bunkers. The German defense of the Scharnhorst Line in this sector was poor due to weak dispositions and the mediocre quality of the inexperienced infantry and fortification troops. There were no appreciable defenses along the river aside from artillery and mortar fire, and the American crossing was uncontested. German artillery had excellent observation posts on the heights overlooking the crossing sites and bunkers, but the shifting of fires was too slow to impede the rapid US advance to the bunker line.

Several of the Westwall
bunkers in Palenberg were
disguised as houses or farm
buildings, such as this
example in the sector of the
119th Infantry Regiment.

The Krinkelterwald

December 16, 1944

BACKGROUND TO BATTLE

The German plans for the Ardennes offensive followed the usual late-war tactics of using infantry divisions to secure the breakthrough of the defenses, followed by Panzer divisions for the breakout and exploitation phase. The *Schwerpunkt* (focal point) of the German assault was the 6. Panzerarmee attack on the right, led by 1. SS-Panzer-Korps. Three infantry divisions were used in the first wave to crack open the American defenses. This section examines the confrontation between elements of 277. Volksgrenadier-Division and the 393rd Infantry Regiment, 99th Division on the first day of the offensive.

277. Volksgrenadier-Division was at about 75–80 percent strength at the start of the Ardennes offensive, but was not well trained or equipped, and had significant shortages of junior officers and NCOs. It was rated at Kampfwert 3: suitable for defense. The division was deployed along the Westwall in the Ardennes in November 1944. The division's mission during the Ardennes offensive was to secure Rollbahn A, a forest trail from Hollerath through the Krinkelterwald (Krinkelt woods) to the road junction of Krinkelt–Rocherath, to take the twin villages, and to proceed toward the Elsenborn Ridge in the direction of Verviers. Two other divisions, 12. Volksgrenadier-Division and 3. Fallschirmjäger-Division, were assigned to secure additional routes farther south to provide 12. SS-Panzer-Division a breakthrough toward the main objective of Liége.

In view of the secrecy attached to the offensive, no reconnaissance was
conducted of American positions by the division, and only the regimental
commanders were given any details of the mission and its objectives. The
division was moved into position on December 14 with Grenadier-Regiment
989 deployed near the Westwall bunkers around Hollerath and Grenadier-
Regiment 990 around Udenbreth. A *Sturmgeschütz* assault-gun brigade was
promised for support but did not arrive in time; a few assault guns arrived on
the evening of December 16, after the attacks had taken place.

Facing 277. Volksgrenadier-Division was the understrength 393rd
Infantry Regiment, with the 3/393rd Infantry on the right opposite Grenadier-
Regiment 989 and the 1/393rd Infantry on the left, opposite
Grenadier-Regiment 990. The 2/393rd Infantry was taking part in an
operation farther north in support of the 2nd Infantry Division, aimed at
securing the Roer River dams. The regiment's parent formation, the 99th
Division, had arrived in the Ardennes in November 1944, and replaced the
9th Division. The 99th Division was deployed in a quiet section of the front
for seasoning, and took over the 9th Division defenses along the international
highway that formed an informal front line. The month the division served
in the line helped to acclimate the division to the surroundings. The 393rd
Infantry Regiment conducted numerous reconnaissance missions into
Germany, and in the days prior to the offensive had conducted a
"demonstration" to distract the Germans from the Roer Dam operation,
including clashes with Grenadier-Regiment 991 on the Rathsberg Hills on the
northern side of the regiment's positions. One of the most important
accomplishments of the division in November was the creation of numerous
reinforced dugouts along the defense lines. These log-reinforced shelters were
intended to shield the troops from artillery strikes in the trees overhead that
sprayed the ground with lethal splinters, a lesson painfully learned in previous
months in the Hürtgenwald fighting farther south.

Two riflemen of the 393rd
Infantry Regiment in the
Krinkelterwald.

MAP KEY

1 **0700hrs:** The German artillery lifts and I./GR 989 overruns two platoons from K/393rd Infantry.

2 **0700hrs:** Grenadier-Regiment 990 starts its initial attack, but the attack is broken by heavy counterfire before it reaches American lines. Grenadier-Regiment 990 renews its attack at 0800hrs and by 0830hrs, begins to overwhelm C/393rd Infantry's forward defenses.

3 **c.0745hrs:** Surviving elements of K/393rd Infantry withdraw back toward the company command post.

4 **0815hrs:** Lt Col Jack Allen orders 2nd Platoon, L/393rd Infantry to withdraw and set up rear defenses, but it is hit hard.

5 **c.0845hrs:** Lt Col Allen orders L/393rd Infantry to shift southward toward this sector.

6 **After 0900hrs:** Oberst Georg Fieger, commanding Grenadier-Regiment 989, attempts to reinvigorate the German attack by sending in II./GR 989 slightly to the right of the original attack, putting further pressure on the 3/393rd Infantry's headquarters.

7 **c.0930hrs:** Grenadier-Regiment 991 attacks from Remscheid to the southwest, hitting the two left-flank platoons of B/393rd Infantry.

8 **1000hrs:** A/393rd Infantry stages a counterattack to reinforce B/393rd Infantry, pushing the Germans back about 300yd.

9 **1015hrs:** The left platoon of C/393rd Infantry is overrun and the company command post comes under attack.

10 **c.1100hrs:** Allen orders I/393rd Infantry to withdraw back to the battalion command post area.

11 **Late morning:** the 393rd Infantry Regiment's minelaying platoon, reinforced by some headquarters troops, stages a bayonet charge near the C/393rd Infantry command post, stabilizing the US defense.

12 **c.1400hrs:** Allen is informed that the regimental HQ is sending in I/394th Infantry as reinforcements.

13 **1600hrs:** I/394th Infantry arrives and manages to stabilize the US defenses.

14 **Late afternoon:** I./SS-PzGrRgt 25 begins to exploit the gap punched in US defenses and reaches the western outskirts of the woods facing Rocherath.

Battlefield environment

The American positions were located in a forested area dominated by pine trees. The German forces advanced over open farm fields toward the forest. The forest in this area had few real roads, but unlike the wild Hürtgenwald, these woods were used for logging. As a result, the forest floor was relatively clear. Many sections of the forest were made up of stands of planted trees in neat rows with little underbrush, which made transit easier. Owing to the logging, there were numerous logging trails and cuts. The weather was typical of early winter in this region with the temperature hovering around freezing, but the ground was not yet frozen deep enough for permanent snow cover. The damp weather alternated between rain and snow, and early-morning fog was common. Snow would sometimes stick in shaded areas but melt in more exposed areas. The autumn had been unusually wet, and as a result, farm fields were usually sodden and impassable for most vehicles.

This is one of the log-reinforced foxholes of the 99th Division in the Krinkelterwald in December 1944. These fighting pits protected the infantry from overhead artillery bursts and the resulting spray of lethal wood splinters.

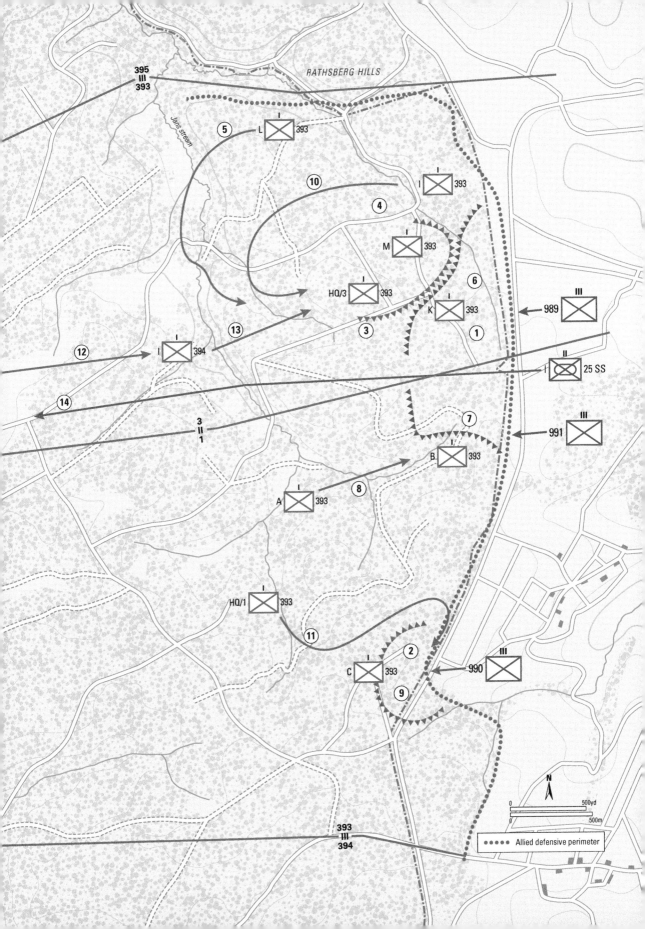

RATHSBERG HILLS

395
III
393

Jans stream

⑤ L ⊠ 393

⑩

④

⊠ 393

M ⊠ 393

⑥

HQ/3 ⊠ 393

K ⊠ 393

③

①

⑬

⑫ I ⊠ 394

3
II
1

⑭

⑦

B ⊠ 393

⑧

A ⊠ 393

HQ/1 ⊠ 393

⑪

C ⊠ 393

②

⑨

989 ⊠ III

II
I ⊠ 25 SS

III
991 ⊠

III
990 ⊠

393
III
394

N

0   500yd
0   500m

●●●● Allied defensive perimeter

INTO COMBAT

Operation *Herbstnebel* ("autumn mist") began in the predawn hours of Saturday, December 16 with a furious artillery barrage of American positions starting at 0530hrs. The artillery strikes began against targets in the American rear and gradually moved forward to strike the tactical defenses near the international highway, finally lifting at around 0700hrs. Searchlights were directed against the low cloud cover to illuminate the woods. The German artillery strikes were very effective in chewing up the field-telephone network between the forward battalions and divisional headquarters, but they were largely ineffective against the forward US defenses due to the detonation of many of the artillery rounds in the tops of the fir trees. The initial artillery strikes in the rear had given the forward American battalions time to take shelter in the covered trenches.

Grenadier-Regiment 989, commanded by Oberst Georg Fieger, set out from the bunkers near Hollerath toward the Schwarzenburch trail. The forest in this area had no real roads, but unlike the wild Hürtgenwald, these woods were used for logging and so had numerous logging trails and cuts, and little underbrush. Owing to the forest conditions, Fieger decided to deploy his two battalions in column, with I./GR 989 leading the attack. The attack began shortly after the artillery lifted and struck the right flank of the 3/393rd Infantry, overrunning two platoons from K/393rd Infantry, and leaving it with only the 1st Platoon and two mortar squads that were surrounded. The company commander, Capt Stephen Plume, reported that "the whole right flank had been swallowed up in the first rush of Germans. Every man was killed or captured." Plume ordered the surviving elements of the company to withdraw back toward the company command post. At 0815hrs the battalion commander, Lt Col Jack Allen, ordered the battalion reserve, the 2nd Platoon of L/393rd Infantry, to withdraw and set up rear defenses, but it was hit hard by advancing German troops and suffered 25 percent casualties in a short skirmish. On learning of this situation, Allen ordered the rest of L/393rd

Riflemen of the 9th Infantry Regiment (2nd Infantry Division) in the Krinkelterwald on December 13, 1944, at the start of yet another offensive against the Roer dams. The presence of this experienced division behind the 99th Division prevented a penetration by 6. Panzerarmee toward the Elsenborn Ridge, a focal point of the Ardennes offensive.

Infantry to shift southward toward this sector. As the company moved to the southeast, it encountered heavy German forces infiltrating through the woods, so instead it headed farther west, then doubled back to enter the defensive belt behind the battalion command post.

By 0915–0930hrs, a significant German force had reached the outskirts of the battalion command post. The headquarters troops, including cooks and clerks, were thrown into the defenses. Reinforcements from L/393rd Infantry arrived at around 1015hrs, but the battalion command post remained surrounded and under intense pressure. Many of the German troops ignored this skirmish and continued to infiltrate toward the objective farther west. At around 1100hrs, Allen ordered I/393rd Infantry to withdraw to the battalion command post. By late morning, the push by I./GR 989 had run out of steam due to heavy casualties, especially among the officers and NCOs. The German troops were inexperienced, and the small-unit leaders attempted to lead by example, resulting in heavy casualties among them. Fieger attempted to reinvigorate the attack by sending in II./GR 989 slightly to the right of the original attack.

Many of the infantry of 277. Volksgrenadier-Division, such as this young officer, were issued winter snow-suits prior to the Ardennes offensive.

At around 1400hrs, Allen was informed that the regiment was sending in I/394th Infantry as reinforcements. The next wave of German attacks flared up again in front of the battalion command post and M/393rd Infantry positions as II./GR 989 pushed forward. M/393rd Infantry, the heavy-weapons company, reported that there were 200–300 German dead in front of its positions. I/394th Infantry arrived at around 1600hrs and managed to stabilize the defenses. The German attacks petered out after 1630hrs, by which time the 3/393rd Infantry's battalion headquarters had re-established field-telephone communications with divisional artillery. Any sign of German activity was met with mortar and artillery fire.

In contrast, the German infantry companies had no means of communication at all, since their radios were not powerful enough to operate in the forest and no field-telephone net had been established. By the end of the day, Grenadier-Regiment 989's attack had collapsed due to heavy casualties, especially among the officers. One battalion commander was dead, the other severely wounded; the regimental commander had collapsed and was evacuated. Some elements of the regiment had advanced more than one mile into the forest, and had reached the Jans stream. However, there was no communication with the advance troops inside the forest. For all intents and purposes, Grenadier-Regiment 989 was no longer combat-effective.

By nightfall, the 3/393rd Infantry had lost about half its troops and was clinging to a shortened defensive perimeter inside the forest around the battalion headquarters and neighboring M/393rd Infantry's positions. German troops were free to infiltrate past it to the north or south. K/393rd Infantry had been reduced to two officers and 45 men from an original strength of about six officers and 185 men; L/393rd Infantry was down to three officers and 130 men; I/393rd Infantry had all six officers and 150 men; M/393rd Infantry had lost its entire 1st Platoon and was down to about 90 men.

In the southern sector of the 393rd Infantry Regiment, Grenadier-Regiment 990 started its initial attack around 0700hrs. The 1/393rd Infantry's defenses were on the forest edge overlooking the international highway with clear fields of fire. The 1/393rd Infantry had continual contact with divisional artillery and the German

To maintain the firepower of *Volksgrenadier* divisions, the intention was to equip them with the new StG 44 assault rifle. However, shortages of the weapon led to continued reliance on the Kar 98k rifle in most units.

attack across open fields was met with fire from infantry heavy weapons and field artillery, breaking the attack before it reached American lines. At the time, B/ and C/393rd Infantry were in the forward defense line, with A/393rd Infantry in reserve. The German attack was renewed at 0800hrs when Generalmajor Wilhelm Viebig, the divisional commander, committed his modest reserves, a *Pionier* company and Füsilier-Kompanie 277. At 0830hrs, C/393rd Infantry reported that the Germans had made penetrations in its defensive line, but that the German forces seemed content to take up defensive positions rather than continue to attack.

In frustration at the lack of success in getting Grenadier-Regiment 990 into the American defenses, Viebig ordered the reserve Grenadier-Regiment 991 to attack from Remscheid to the southwest, hitting two platoons of B/393rd Infantry at around 0930hrs. The sudden infusion of another German regiment succeeded in overrunning the two left platoons of B/393rd Infantry. The battalion commander, Maj Matthew Legler, ordered the reserve, A/393rd Infantry, to restore the situation. It staged a counterattack at around 1000hrs, pushing back the Germans about 300yd. However, the attack stalled under heavy German artillery fire and the arrival of additional German infantry. Nevertheless, this section of the front was stabilized.

In the south, the left platoon of C/393rd Infantry was finally overrun at around 1015hrs, and the company command post came under attack. C/393rd Infantry requested reinforcements, but all that was available was the regimental minelaying platoon. Reinforced by some headquarters troops, about 40 men staged a bayonet charge near the C/393rd Infantry company command post, temporarily stabilizing the defense. By the end of the day, the

Troops of the headquarters of the 393rd Infantry Regiment (99th Division) during the Ardennes fighting in the winter of 1944/45.

Counterattack in the Krinkelterwald

Around 1100hrs, the command post of C/393rd Infantry on the far right flank of the regiment's positions was on the verge of being overrun by another surge from Grenadier-Regiment 990 and Füsilier-Kompanie 277. The only available reserve was the minelaying platoon of the regimental Anti-Tank Company, consisting of Lt Harry Parker and 25 men. These men were organized under the 1/393rd Infantry's S-3, 1/Lt Lawrence Duffin, who rounded up 13 more men from the battalion headquarters company for the counterattack. The US force moved through the woods along the C/393rd Infantry supply road and then used the open ground of the international highway as a line of departure for a quicker advance on the objective.

On approaching the beleaguered command post through the woods, Duffin noticed large numbers of German troops, estimated at about three companies. Significantly outnumbered, Duffin decided to use the element of surprise and – along with Parker – ordered the men to fix bayonets. "Yelling like Indians on a dead run, bayonets leveled," the surprise bayonet charge through the woods led to a mêlée around the bunkers and dugouts of the company command post. The attack killed 28 German troops and relieved the command post. Duffin's counterattack force then took up defensive positions to restore the US defense lines.

1/393rd Infantry lines were near their original position, though with inroads on the right and left ends; 277. Volksgrenadier-Division was exhausted, after suffering very heavy casualties. Grenadier-Regiment 990 alone had lost about 350 men killed and 580 wounded in action.

The commander of 12. SS-Panzer-Division, SS-Standartenführer Hugo Kraas, looked on in frustration through the morning of December 16 as wave after wave of infantry from 277. Volksgrenadier-Division failed to achieve any significant penetration into the American defenses. Feeling pressure to get his troops moving, around noon Kraas ordered I./SS-PzGrRgt 25, led by SS-Hauptsturmführer Alfons Ott, to exploit the gap in the American defenses secured by Grenadier-Regiment 989 in the northern sector. The Waffen-SS battalion advanced through the woods during the afternoon against little opposition; accompanying antitank and infantry-gun platoons stalled when their prime movers became stuck in the mud in the forest tracks. They encountered no troops from Grenadier-Regiment 989, and reached the western side of the forest facing Rocherath. Ott had no communication with either regimental or divisional headquarters due to poor radio performance in the woods, so he sent a runner back to coordinate further actions. However, his unit was spotted by American observers in Rocherath and brought under artillery fire, with the result that Ott pulled his battalion back into the woods and set up a defensive perimeter for the night.

The failure of 277. Volksgrenadier-Division to penetrate the American defenses in the Krinkelterwald on December 16 was one of the many small reasons for the failure of the Ardennes offensive. The attack involved seven German infantry battalions against two American battalions. The US side had the advantage of well-constructed defenses within a forest that proved resistant to artillery fire. German armored support in the form of the promised assault guns might have helped overcome the American defenses, especially in the southern sector where the defenses were accessible via the open ground near the international highway, but the problems facing 277. Volksgrenadier-Division were more than just the lack of armored support.

In contrast, the *Volksgrenadier-Divisionen* of 5. Panzerarmee to the south did manage to penetrate the American forest defenses of the 106th Division on December 16 without armored support. The difference was tactics. Dietrich's 6. Panzerarmee followed Berlin's instructions and avoided tactical reconnaissance of the American defenses, and employed a heavy artillery barrage at the outset of the attack. In contrast, Manteuffel's 5. Panzerarmee ignored Berlin's instructions; Manteuffel personally carried out reconnaissance missions to gain an impression of American defenses. He quickly concluded that the opening artillery barrage would be ineffective against troops in strongpoints within a forest, and would simply alert the enemy infantry to take shelter. Instead, he insisted that the *Volksgrenadier-Divisionen* depend upon infiltration of the thinly spread American defenses rather than upon the artillery to soften them up – a classic German infantry tactic since 1918. Tactical clumsiness, poor-quality troops, and a lack of armored support all helped to undermine the 277. Volksgrenadier-Division attack on December 16.

On December 17, following the failure of 277. Volksgrenadier-Division and its neighboring infantry divisions, 12. SS-Panzer-Division took matters into its own hands and attempted to conduct the breakthrough using *Panzergrenadiere* with tank support. This contradicted German tactical doctrine which recognized that a stout infantry defense should be penetrated before the injection of the exploitation force. 6. Panzerarmee felt that this doctrine had to be ignored in order to maintain the intended pace of the offensive. The American infantry defenses had not been broken, and on December 17, the 393rd Infantry Regiment withdrew into Krinkelt–Rocherath with the assistance of reinforcements from the neighboring 2nd Infantry Division. This resulted in the battle for Krinkelt–Rocherath over the next several days that gutted 12. SS-Panzer-Division. Combined with the failure of 1. SS-Panzer Division to the south, 6. Panzerarmee failed to win a breakthrough at the focal point of its attack, thus dooming the Ardennes offensive.

Following the fighting in the Krinkelterwald and the battle for the twin villages of Krinkelt–Rocherath, the 393rd Infantry Regiment withdrew to the northwest to the Elsenborn Ridge, where elements of the regiment are shown setting up new defensive positions on December 20, 1944.

Analysis

One of the Palenberg bunkers knocked out during the October 2 fighting covered in this book. The distinctive spall pattern of a bazooka hit can be seen above the embrasure.

The US Army infantry of World War II was a far more modern force than their German counterparts, with numerous advantages in firepower and mobility and substantially higher combat power. German propaganda depicted the US infantry as casualty-averse, too dependent on the supporting arms of tanks and artillery, and too reliant on material superiority. All of this is true; but it would have been strange if the US Army did not exploit its advantages to overwhelm its opponent.

The intended armament of the *Volksgrenadier* divisions was the StG 44 assault rifle. However, production in 1944 was too limited to meet demand, and it remained a relatively rare weapon at the time of the Ardennes offensive.

LESSONS LEARNED: THE GERMANS

Regardless of any lessons learned, the German infantry faced inexorable manpower, training, and equipment problems. The commitment of many NCO schools and training divisions to the front in the autumn of 1944 consumed the "seed" of future divisions; and the temporary glut of able young troops from the Luftwaffe and Kriegsmarine in the autumn of 1944 had largely ended by the winter of 1944/45. Desperate situations demanded desperate measures, so more and more infantry divisions were filled out with the bottom scrapings of personnel. Aside from hastily trained conscripts, the infantry was filled out from local *Landesschützen* (regional militias) made up of 55–60-year-old men, and *Alarmheiten* (emergency units) made up of rear-area noncombatant troops. The Heer formations were supplemented by Volkssturm units. The Volkssturm was a pet project of Reich Minister for Propaganda Joseph Goebbels to create a Nazi Party militia with political fervor to overcome the lack of training and weapons. While the Volkssturm showed some promise in eastern Germany, its performance in western Germany was awful. The Volkssturm concept was generally opposed by the Heer as a waste of weapons. Since the local population had already been thoroughly combed for troops, the Volkssturm was recruited either from boys too young for conscription, or old men whom the Heer felt were of little use in uniform, even in the marginally useful *Landesschützen* battalions. To sour the whole idea further for the Heer, the Volkssturm units were under the command of local political authorities, the local *Kreisleiter*, which made them even less useful in defense.

One remaining crutch for the Heer was the extensive fortification effort along the frontier undertaken in the West-Stellung program. Poorly trained troops performed better from prepared defensive positions than in open field conditions, and this helped reduced their vulnerability to the ample American field artillery.

US personnel conducted extensive practice with special weapons prior to the attack on the Scharnhorst Line, including training with the M1A1 flamethrower. In reality, German Westwall bunkers were well protected against remote flamethrower attack such as this, and it was usually necessary for the crew to get up against the bunker wall and fire directly into an embrasure or through an open door.

BELOW A US infantry captain holds a meeting with his platoon commanders during the fighting near Saint-Lô on July 15, 1944. The white vertical strip on the back of the helmet of the nearest lieutenant indicated an officer; a horizontal stripe indicated an NCO. Note the SCR-536 "handie-talkie" radio on his shoulder.

LESSONS LEARNED: THE AMERICANS

The US Army avoided making any systematic changes in the infantry division in 1945, waiting until the conclusion of the war for the General Board to examine improvements. At the small-unit level, the recommendations of the General Board were modest. The plan to add a further BAR to each squad was squashed in 1945, but adopted prior to the Korean War. An assault section with six 2.35in bazookas was added to the Weapons Platoon, mainly due to their value in attacking fortifications rather than their intended antitank role. New weapons were also recommended, leading eventually to the replacement of the M1 Garand with the M14 automatic rifle, and the BAR with the M60 light machine gun. Although organizational changes in the infantry division were modest, there was considerably more attention paid to the need for more realistic training.

At divisional level, tank support had proven vital in combined-arms warfare. Rather than temporarily attaching separate tank battalions to the infantry division, the tanks became organic. Since the tank-destroyer concept was rejected after the war, the scale of tanks in the division went from a battalion to a regiment. The US infantry divisions deployed to Korea in 1950 were not markedly different to those in combat in 1945, but in the ensuing years, far more dramatic changes would take place with the advent of the nuclear battlefield.

Aftermath

In the wake of the Ardennes offensive, the Heer in the West was in a death spiral to defeat. The campaigns from the summer of 1944 to the beginning of 1945 had been enormously costly to the Heer, with a total of 2.2 million casualties from June 1944 to January 10, 1945. Of these, 1.3 million casualties had been suffered on the Eastern Front, and about 795,000 in the West. This was more than double the monthly toll of casualties compared to previous years of the conflict. The defeat of the Ardennes offensive in January 1945 was followed by the renewed Red Army offensive on the Oder–Vistula Front in Poland, approaching Berlin by early February 1945. Priority went to units destined for the Eastern Front.

The German infantry divisions in 1945 avoided the collapse of morale seen in the German Army of 1918. Their defensive efforts remained tenacious to the very end. Nevertheless, the infantry divisions in the West in 1944–45 were a pale shadow of the German infantry divisions at their prime in 1940–42. They had little or no offensive power, and were seldom rated at a combat value above 3.

The 1943–44 decisions to limit the US Army to 90 divisions proved unfortunate in view of the Army's extensive commitments in both Europe and the Pacific. The focus of the US Army after the Ardennes campaign was to maintain the infantry divisions at full strength. The US Army had seriously underestimated the casualty rates likely to be endured in the ETO, so there was a perpetual shortage of trained riflemen. However, this was not comparable in any respect to the German dilemma, since the US Army still had a surplus of technical specialists in the ETO from other branches who could be hastily converted to infantry. In addition, General Dwight D. Eisenhower authorized the formation of volunteer infantry platoons from segregated black service units in the ETO, with the first being deployed after training in March 1945. While this had little immediate impact on the manpower problem, it had a substantial impact on the course of desegregation in the US military.

OPPOSITE The German infantry divisions in the autumn of 1944 were fleshed out using Luftwaffe and Kriegsmarine personnel who had been stranded by the growing fuel shortage. This young soldier, captured during the Aachen campaign, was a former S-Boot (E-Boat) torpedoman. By the autumn of 1944, the Wehrmacht was increasingly unable to support and sustain its infantry divisions in the field. The elite units – the Panzer and *Panzergrenadier* divisions and the troops of the politicized Waffen-SS – had higher priority for manpower and equipment.

UNIT ORGANIZATIONS

German

The *Volksgrenadier-Division* had two patterns of infantry regiments: a bicycle-mobile type (*Grenadier-Regiment auf Fahrrädern*) and a conventional type. The principal difference was that the mobile variant had 698 bicycles instead of the usual 100. The *Grenadier-Regiment* totaled 1,854 men compared to the 1943 pattern with 2,008 men.

The *Grenadier-Regiment* consisted of a headquarters and headquarters company (*Stabs, Stabskompanie*), two *Grenadier-Bataillonen*, an infantry-gun company (*Infanteriegeschütz-Kompanie*) with six 7.5cm and two 15cm infantry guns, and a tank-destroyer company (*Panzerjäger-Kompanie*). The *Panzerjäger-Kompanie*, traditionally called 14. Kompanie, had six 7.5cm PaK 40 towed guns and 36 *Panzerschreck* antitank rocket launchers; the 1944 pattern dispensed with the towed guns and had 72 rocket launchers. The *Grenadier-Bataillon* was smaller than the 1943-pattern battalion: 642 versus 708 men. It consisted of a headquarters company, a support platoon, three grenadier companies, and a heavy-weapons company with six 8cm mortars and four 7.5cm infantry guns.

The German infantry company was originally called a rifle company (*Schützenkompanie*) through the December 1943 KStN 131n. This configuration had a headquarters (*Kompanietrupp*), three rifle platoons (*Züge*), an 8cm mortar platoon, and a train (*Tross*) and numbered 147 officer and men, 27 horses, 99 rifles, 16 light machine guns, and two 8cm mortars. Under the September 1944 KStN 131V *Volksgrenadier* configuration, it was renamed as a *Grenadier-Kompanie*. This configuration was based around a company headquarters and three platoons (*Züge*), but dropped the mortar section and train for a total of 119 men, 10 horses, 46 rifles, 54 assault rifles, and nine light machine guns. Each platoon had a headquarters (*Zugtrupp*) and three squads (*Gruppen*). There was a total of four NCOs, 29 men, and three horses per platoon; only 1. Zug had an officer. Two light machine guns were held in the *Zugtrupp* and the other was deployed with 3. Gruppe; in practice, the older pattern was usually followed with one MG 34 or MG 42 light machine gun in each *Gruppe* for a total of three per *Zug* and nine per *Kompanie*. The authorized armament for 1. Zug and 2. Zug was five Kar 98k rifles and 26 StG 44 assault rifles; 3. Zug had 20 Kar 98k rifles and nine MP 40 submachine guns.

American

The US Army infantry regiment was organized under T/O&E 7-11 with modifications in February 1944 and again in June 1944. Its essential components were a headquarters and headquarters company, three infantry battalions, a cannon company, antitank company, service company, and medical detachment, totaling 3,100 officers and men. The cannon company was armed with six 105mm M3 howitzers, a smaller and lighter weapon than the 105mm M2A1 howitzer used in the division's field artillery battalions. The antitank company had nine 57mm M1 antitank guns. The 2.36in bazooka rocket launcher was distributed throughout the regiment as a self-defense weapon, though often allotted to the rifle platoons as an assault weapon.

The infantry battalion totaled 825 men and 40 vehicles under the June 30, 1944 modification. It consisted of a headquarters and headquarters company, three rifle companies, and a heavy-weapons company. The heavy-weapons company had three mortar sections with two 81mm mortar sections each for a total of six 81mm mortars, and two machine-gun sections with two squads each with a total of four .30-caliber machine guns.

The rifle company had 187 men including six officers. It consisted of a company headquarters, three rifle platoons, and a weapons platoon with two .30-caliber light machine guns and three 60mm mortars. Each rifle platoon had one officer and 40 enlisted men; it consisted of a headquarters and three rifle squads. Each squad consisted of 12 men: a squad leader, assistant leader, BAR rifleman, BAR assistant, BAR ammunition bearer, and seven riflemen.

OPPOSITE German troops inspect some captured US Army infantry gear during the Cotentin fighting in the summer of 1944.

BIBLIOGRAPHY

A NOTE ON SOURCES

I chose the three skirmishes presented in the book based on the availability of documentation on both sides. I intentionally avoided a skirmish from the Hürtgenwald battles as the Rush book provides such an exemplary example of a comparative study. I also intentionally avoided any 1945 skirmishes due to the severe degradation of German infantry by that point. On the US side, the best source for small-unit actions is the "Combat Interview" collection in Record Group 407 at the National Archives and Records Administration (NARA II) at College Park, Maryland. These offer more detail than the after-action reports, also in RG 407. On the German side, published accounts are almost totally lacking and so the accounts in the Foreign Military Studies (FMS) series are invaluable, though patchy. German divisional reports in the West in 1944 are extremely uneven due to the loss of so many unit records. I mainly relied on the extensive microfilm collection in RG 242 at NARA. Of the three skirmishes here, RG 242 coverage of the Montebourg fighting was fair, coverage of the Palenberg fighting was good, and coverage of the Ardennes fighting was poor.

The comparative performance of German and American infantry in 1944–45 has been the subject of considerable controversy. In the Vietnam War years of the 1960s and 1970s, several revisionist historians including Trevor Dupuy and Martin van Creveld offered a dismissive portrait of US Army performance while portraying the German infantry as a model of defensive stamina. These views found a receptive audience not only because of the antimilitary sentiments of the day, but because the US Army was itself trying to determine how to fight outnumbered and win in a possible confrontation with the Soviet Army in Central Europe. The Wehrmacht of World War II seemed to offer a worthwhile model. This eventually resulted in a backlash, spearheaded by a number of younger US Army officers such as Bonn, Brown, Mansoor, and Doubler, many of whom served in the history department of the US Military Academy at West Point. I had the privilege of hearing these officers firsthand at the many presentations to the New York Military Affairs Symposium in the 1980s. There has been a considerable renaissance in studies of the US Army in 1944–45, but coverage of the German infantry divisions remains poor. Most English-language books cover the German elite formations at the expense of the more mundane infantry formations; German-language accounts of the war in the West in 1944–45 remain scarce.

US ARMY FOREIGN MILITARY STUDIES

Fieger, Georg. *The 989th Grenadier Regiment, 14–17 December 1944* (B-025).

Hechler, Lucian. *The Germans Opposite XIX Corps* (R-21).

Keil, Günther. *Grenadier Regiment 919, Kampfgruppe Keil* (C-018).

Keil, Günther. *Infantry Regiment 1058 and Kampfgruppe Keil* (B-844).

Lange, Wolfgang. *183. Volksgrenadier Division Sept 1944–25 Jan 1945* (B-753).

Macholz, Siegfried. *49. Infanterie Division* (B-792).

Mauer, E. *243rd Infantry Division Operations against American Army Troops 5 June to 30 June 1944* (D-382).

Schlieben, Karl-Wilhelm. *709th Infantry Division, Dec 1943–30 Jun 1944* (B-845).

Viebig, Wilhelm. *Commitment of the 277th Volksgrenadier Division, November and December 1944* (B-273).

US GOVERNMENT REPORTS

Drea, Edward (1983). *Unit Reconstitution: A Historical Perspective*. US Army Combat Studies Institute: December 1983.

Gorman, Paul (1992). *The Secret of Future Victories*. Institute for Defense Analyses: February 1992.

Stockfisch, J.A. (1975). *Models, Data, and War: A Critique of the Study of Conventional Forces*. Rand Corporation: March 1975.

Wainstein, Leonard (1986). *The Relationship of Battle Damage to Unit Combat Performance.* Institute for Defense Analyses: April 1986.

Wainstein, Leonard (1973). *Rates of Advance in Infantry Division Attacks in the Normandy Campaign– Northern France and Siegfried Line Campaigns.* Institute for Defense Analyses: December 1973.

Wainstein, Leonard (1973). *Some Allied and German Casualty Rates in the European Theater of Operations.* Institute for Defense Analyses: December 1973.

Breaching the Siegfried Line: XIX Corps, US Army 2 October 1944. US Army: 1945.

Handbook on German Military Forces 1945 TM-E 30-451. US War Department: March 15, 1945, reprinted by Louisiana State University Press: 1990. *Operational Data for Selected Field Artillery Units during World War II and the Korean War.* Stanford Research Institute: June 1954.

Organization, Equipment and Tactical Employment of the Infantry Divisions. General Board, USFET: 1945.

Personnel Attrition Rates in Historical Land Combat Operations: An Annotated Bibliography. US Army Concepts Analysis Agency: June 1993.

The Value of Field Fortifications in Modern Warfare, Vol. 1. Defense Nuclear Agency: December 1979.

BOOKS AND ARTICLES

Andrew, Stephen (2011). *German Army Grenadier 1944–45.* Glasgow: Landser.

Balkoski, Joseph (2005). *Utah Beach: The Amphibious Landing and Airborne Operations on D-Day, June 6, 1944.* Mechanicsburg, PA: Stackpole.

Bellanger, Yves (2002). *US Army Infantry Divisions 1943–45: Volume 1 – Organization, Doctrine and Equipment.* Solihull: Helion.

Bonn, Keith (1994). *When the Odds were Even: The Vosges Mountains Campaign, October 1944–January 1945.* Novato, CA: Presidio.

Bradley, Omar (1951). *A Soldier's Story.* New York, NY: Henry Holt.

Brown, John Sloan (1985). "Colonel Trevor N. Dupuy and the Myths of Wehrmacht Superiority: A Reconsideration," *Military Affairs,* January 1985: 16–20.

Castillo, Jasen (2014). *Endurance and War: The National Sources of Military Cohesion.* Stanford, CA: Stanford University Press.

Cavanagh, William (2004). *The Battle East of Elsenborn & The Twin Villages.* Barnsley: Pen & Sword.

Comparato, Frank (1965). *Age of Great Guns.* Harrisburg, PA: Stackpole.

van Creveld, Martin (1982). *Fighting Power: German and US Army Performance 1939–1945.* Westport, CT: Greenwood.

Doubler, Michael (1994). *Closing with the Enemy: How GIs Fought the War in Europe 1944–45.* Lawrence, KS: University Press of Kansas.

Dunn, Walter (2012). "German Bodenstandig Divisions," in Sanders Marble, ed., *Scraping the Barrel: The Military Use of Substandard Manpower 1860–1960.* New York, NY: Fordham University Press.

Dunn, Walter, Jr. (2003). *Heroes or Traitors?: The German Replacement Army, the July Plot, and Adolf Hitler.* Westport, CT: Praeger.

Dupuy, Trevor (1979). *Numbers, Predictions & War.* London: Macdonald and Jane's.

Gross, Manfred (2008). *Westwällkampfe – Die Angriffe der Amerikaner 1944/45 zwischen Ormont und Geilenkirchen.* Aachen: Helios.

Hewitt, Robert (1946). *Work Horse of the Western Front: The Story of the 30th Infantry Division.* Washington, DC: Infantry Journal Press.

Jordan, Kelly (2002). "Right for the Wrong Reason: S.L.A. Marshall and the Ratio of Fire in Korea," *Journal of Military History,* January 2002: 135–62.

Lauer, Walter (1985). *Battle Babies: The Story of the 99th Infantry Division in World War II.* Nashville, TN: Battery Press.

Mansoor, Peter (1999). *The GI Offensive in Europe: The Triumph of American Infantry Divisions, 1941–45.* Lawrence, KS: University Press of Kansas.

Marshall, S.L.A. (1947). *Men against Fire: The Problem of Battle Command.* Gloucester, MA: Peter Smith.

Rush, Robert (2001). *Hell in Hürtgen Forest: The Ordeal and Triumph of an American Infantry Regiment.* Lawrence, KS: University Press of Kansas.

Rusiecki, Stephen (1996). *The Key to the Bulge: The Battle for Losheimergraben.* Westport, CT: Praeger.

Shils, Edward & Morris Janowitz (1948). "Cohesion and Disintegration in the Wehrmacht in World War II," *Public Opinion Quarterly,* Summer 1948: 284.

Tholhte, Karl (1945). "A German Reflects Upon Artillery," *Field Artillery Journal,* December 1945: 709–15.

Wijers, Hans (2009). *The Battle of the Bulge: Vol.1, The Losheim Gap/Holding the Line.* Mechanicsburg, PA: Stackpole.

INDEX

References to plates are shown in **bold** with captions in brackets.